Don't Believe The Hype Of The Negative Media

10 Reasons Why The Future Is Brighter Than You Think

BY
COACH MICHAEL TAYLOR

Published by Creation Publishing Group LLC
www.creationpublishing.com
© 2020 Michael Taylor
ISBN # 978-0-9969487-84
Library of Congress Number # 2019902101

All rights reserved. No part of this book may be used or reproduced, stored in, or introduced into, a retrieval system, or transmitted in any form or by any means without the express written consent of the publisher.

Published and printed in the United States of America.

Contents

Foreword by Robert White v

Acknowledgements vii

Introduction 1

Chapter 1: Being Human 5

Chapter 2: Divine Intelligence & Evolution 41

Chapter 3: Spirituality 59

Chapter 4: Race 71

Chapter 5: Factfulness 83

Chapter 6: Love 101

Chapter 7: Health 123

Chapter 8: Wealth 135

Chapter 9: Education 147

Chapter 10: Technology 157

What's Next? 171

Bio 175

Foreword
by Robert White

I'VE BEEN AN entrepreneur building companies that provide high-impact experiential training and executive coaching for over forty years. Over one million people have graduated from programs designed, sold and delivered by companies I've founded and led: Lifespring, Inc., ARC International and Extraordinary People.

Michael's work is aligned with mine and learning about his history was fascinating and engaging. We've traded ideas, done some mutual problem-solving and just enjoyed getting to know each other. In addition to the friendship, I hold him as representing the next generation of effective transformational coaches and trainers so it is my obligation to share with him anything I can.

Michael and I have similar life experiences though his seem both unique and more challenging than mine. We both had strong, influential mothers who taught us the power of taking responsibility for our own lives. He was raised in poverty as was I. He had five siblings; I had three. We were both taught that the future was up to us and that it could be better than the one we were born into.

His recent successes—and there are many—are built on the learnings from his significant failures earlier in his adult life; that is one of the reasons I love and respect him. His obvious brilliance and accomplishments are balanced by what he has learned from those failures; by his humility and practicality. Much was said about President Obama being a good guy to have a beer with. Michael shares that quality. He's truly a good man as a husband, father and quality contributor to so many lives through his books and coaching.

In this book you'll have an experience somewhat like a quality buffet with lots of variety. By quality I mean the kind of buffet a five-star hotel puts out at a fairly high price. You know the kind: fresh sushi, a standing rib roast, Virginia honey ham, five kinds of vegetables each prepared a different way … mouth-watering and satisfying in every way. By variety I mean you can pick and choose based on your appetite, your needs.

The buffet choices here include enrolling you in the possibility of writing your own script for the movie of your life; of getting in touch with your essential life energy and harnessing it for abundance and joy.

Michael doesn't hide from a current reality that includes much racial tension. His point of view is that the majority of Americans—of all skin colors—are not racist. Yet, we must pay attention to discrimination and the mindsets that help us move past any limiting beliefs.

Ultimately, living the life we were born to live depends on our ability to give and receive love. It's been the heart of my teaching and executive coaching and you're going to be challenged by Michael's wisdom in this important life come-from and skill set. He'll also touch on creating a sustainable environment, our health, our educational system, the entertainment world and the increasing impact of technology on our families, work and communities.

If you've read this far you'll have gotten a sense of what I mean by a "quality buffet." This is a great book. Enjoy and learn!

Robert White

Author of "Living an Extraordinary Life," Executive Coach and Leadership Trainer. www.TheRobertWhite.com

Acknowledgements

First, foremost, and always, I must acknowledge the Divine Energy and Intelligence that created and is still creating this amazing Universe we live in. This Divine Intelligence goes by many names, God, Yahweh, Great Spirit, The Universe, and a wide variety of other names. Ultimately, these are just labels we use to try to comprehend the incomprehensible, yet the names we use to try to define it are irrelevant; what's important is that we develop an intimacy and connection with this power that is greater than ourselves. I feel truly blessed to have created this intimacy and connection with this Divine Intelligence and I have come to know that I am simply a divine expression of it. Therefore, it is with great humility that I acknowledge and give thanks for my connection to this Divine Intelligence.

If there is something called a resiliency gene I definitely inherited it from my mom Geneva who is the epitome of the optimistic thinker. As I think back over the adversities and challenges she had to overcome as a single mom with six children back in the '60s, I am inspired beyond words by her ability to "figure things out" and overcome any obstacle. Despite the fact that we could have been considered the poster children for poverty, my mom instilled in me at a very young age that if I wanted something badly enough, no one or no thing could keep me from attaining it except myself. She always encouraged me to dream big and not put any limitations on myself. In retrospect, I cannot remember a single time when she spoke negatively about her situation or blamed anyone for her circumstances. She simply found a way to make things happen by taking complete responsibility for her life and her children.

Everything I am is the result of her love, guidance, and leading by example and I am forever indebted to her for the man I have become. Thanks for everything, Mom; I told you I was going to make an impact on the world. I love you more than love!

In my early 20s I read a book by Dr. Wayne Dyer that literally changed my life. In the book he stated, "As a human being you have within you the capacity to do anything any other human being has done, and if it hasn't been done, you can be the first." As a young black male with only an 11th grade education, I somehow incorporated this way of thinking into my life and it allowed me to far exceed what society says a young black uneducated male should have been able to accomplish. It was the lessons I learned from Dr. Dyer that challenged me to think deeply about human potential and what human beings are capable of. Throughout my 30s Dr. Dyer became my mentor and motivator and I became positively obsessed with his teachings. I read most of his books, attended several of his lectures and even had the opportunity to meet him at one of his lectures and tell him how much his teachings had impacted my life. After I'd shared my admiration for him and his work, he embraced me and said, "Just remember, I am not the source of your power, you are. Know that there is a Divine Intelligence in you which gives you your power. Learn to trust it and it will guide you to your ultimate destiny." He then embraced me and wished me good luck on this amazing journey called life. I'll never forget his loving hug and warmth. His body emanated this amazing energy, which I felt physically and spiritually. He autographed my book and as I walked away, I knew I had been embraced by a master teacher and when I got home that was exactly what I wrote below his signature. Although Dr. Dyer is no longer with us, his spirit lives on through me and the millions of people whose lives he touched. I am forever grateful for the amazing human being that he was and I will never forget the amazing life lessons I learned from him.

Rest in Paradise, Dr. Dyer, I love you and I miss you!

A few years ago, I ran across a YouTube video titled The Joy of Stats by a Swedish physician, academic, and public speaker named Hans Rosling (July 27, 1948 – February 7, 2017). To be honest, I really dislike statistics, but this video changed my mind. I was intrigued by the graphical nature of the video in which the presenter was explaining why the world was actually getting better and not worse through a series of visually stunning graphics displays. As I watched the video, I was filled with hope and optimism about the future of humanity and the video confirmed what I have always believed to be true; there has never been a better time to be alive on the planet than right now! In his book *Factfulness*, Mr. Rosling provides verifiable facts and statistics that support my beliefs and his book provided me with insights and inspiration that are the basis for this book. Although I will not have the opportunity to meet Mr. Rosling, I wanted to acknowledge him for his brilliant mind, engaging speaking style, and scientific approach to explaining why the future is brighter than most people believe. I highly recommend his book!

As an entrepreneur, it's important to have mentors and teachers to guide us along the entrepreneurial journey. One of my favorite mentors is Peter Diamandis. His groundbreaking book, *The Future Is Faster Than You Think*, provides a high-octane motivational glimpse of what's in store for humanity in the future, and after reading his book, I am even more excited about where we are headed as a human species. Like myself, Peter is committed to providing insights and inspiration to people who are blazing new trails for the future and he focuses on empowering entrepreneurs because he believes they hold the keys to transforming the world and I couldn't agree more. Thank you, Peter, for challenging me to have an *Abundance* mindset, to be *Bold* in my thinking and to know with absolute certainty that *The Future Is Faster Than You Think*.

Now more than ever, the world needs leaders who are open-minded and open-hearted and are committed to building organizations and movements that propel humanity forward. One such leader is Vishen Lakhiani. Vishen is the founder of Mindvalley, which is an organization that teaches you the things that actually matter most in life. And they do it by bringing in the latest cutting-edge techniques, the world's best teachers, and a powerful learning platform that is the best of its kind in the world. In his latest book, *The Buddha and the Badass*, he brings forth a new evolved way of being a leader and he encourages us to redefine what a true leader looks like. I definitely concur with his philosophy and ways of thinking and have incorporated a lot of his teachings into my own life and business. Be sure to check out his book *The Code of the Extraordinary Mind*.

Last, but definitely not least, I would be remiss if I didn't acknowledge you, the reader, for reading this book. If you're reading these words right now, rest assured that I truly appreciate you taking the time to read this book and joining me in spreading some hope and optimism for the future. Because of you, my message will spread and when enough people embrace this positive message of change, the world can and will be transformed for the better.

So, remember the thoughtful words of Margaret Mead, "Never doubt that a small group of thoughtful, committed citizens can change the world. Indeed, it is the only thing that ever has."

Let's go out there and change the world!

Introduction

Today is September 19th 2020 and currently the world is dealing with massive wildfires in California, a recent hurricane that landed on the Gulf Coast and another one being formed in the Gulf as I write this, racial unrest and protests as a result of police brutality, a Covid-19 pandemic that has taken tens of thousands of lives and caused a collapse of the American economy, and the threat of global warming. It's no wonder the majority of people on the planet are pessimistic about the future of humanity.

So, what about you? Are you optimistic or pessimistic about the future?

Since you're reading this book I am going to assume you are optimistic. Or maybe you're pessimistic yet you are looking for reasons to become optimistic. Either way, you've come to the right place. So, let me begin by stating clearly and succinctly that I am an irrepressible optimist who believes there has never been a better time to be alive on this planet than right now.

I am acutely aware of all of the aforementioned challenges and in no way do I want to minimize or deny they exist. However, despite these challenges, I am absolutely certain there are a lot more reasons to be optimistic than pessimistic, and since I know I have the power to choose my mindset and outlook, I choose to focus on the positive and therefore my experiences reflect my positive outlook.

The intention of this book is not to convince you to embrace my point of view. The intention is to give you an opportunity to possibly see the world through a different perspective and if you resonate with some of the ideas in this book and they help you shift from a negative to a more positive outlook, then my intention will be fulfilled and we will both benefit from the information contained in this book.

In no way do I claim to have all the answers, nor do I claim to be an "expert". I am simply an ordinary guy who made a choice to create an extraordinary life. I would like to share some of the insights and lessons I've learned that allowed me to overcome being a high school dropout, divorce, bankruptcy, foreclosure, depression and being homeless for two years living out of my car. I am now an entrepreneur, author of nine books, a motivational speaker, and radio and TV host, which I believe gives me the credibility and the credentials to write this book.

So, here's something for you to think about as you read this book.

Have you ever watched a movie and absolutely loved it? You loved it so much you shared it with a close friend and insisted that they watch it. After they watched it, they absolutely hated it. You couldn't understand why they hated it and they couldn't understand why you loved it. Why is that?

The answer may appear to be complicated, but it is actually pretty simple. The movie isn't actually happening on the screen. The movie is happening within you. In other words, our thoughts, beliefs and feelings are triggered by what we see on the screen. Since each person has had different experiences in life, the images and storylines of the movie reactivate our thoughts, feelings and beliefs based on our own life experiences. If the movie triggers positive memories and beliefs we will generally love it; if it triggers negative memories or beliefs, or no feelings at all, then we probably will not like the movie.

Think of your life like a movie. You are a character in this amazing movie called life. You get to decide whether you will love the movie or hate it based on your thoughts, feelings and beliefs about life.

You are the director and the star of the movie, and you get to write your own script. It's entirely up to you to decide how the story goes and how it will end.

So what story are you going to write?

My hope is by the time you finish reading this book you will be ready to write your own positive story. All stories include challenges and adversities as well as victories and triumphs, so be prepared to include these in your life story. Rest assured that you have everything you need to create your masterpiece, but it all begins with a positive mental attitude and a powerful vision and intention to create an extraordinary story.

It's time for you to create your Oscar-winning movie. Are you ready to write it and live it? This book will provide some insights that I am absolutely certain will assist you in scripting the perfect movie; the only thing that's missing is your commitment to writing your own story and then sharing it with the world.

Are you committed?

Good luck! I'll see you at the Oscars of your life!

"You are not a human being having a spiritual experience. You are a spiritual being having a human experience."

Dr. Wayne Dyer

CHAPTER 1
Being Human

HAVE YOU EVER truly taken the time to think about what it means to be a human being? Is the purpose of being human to follow cultural and societal rules that say the goal is to get a good education, find a career, work hard, build a family, raise your kids, save some money, and then wait for the societal safety valve called retirement?

Is that all life and being human is supposed to be about? Is that all there is to being human?

According to the Associated Press in an article posted on their website,

2020 has been rough on the American psyche. Folks in the U.S. are more unhappy today than they've been in nearly 50 years.

This bold — yet unsurprising — conclusion comes from the COVID Response Tracking Study, *conducted by* NORC *at the University of Chicago. It finds that just 14% of American adults say they're very happy, down from 31% who said the same in 2018. That year, 23% said they'd often or sometimes felt isolated in recent weeks. Now, 50% say that.*

The survey, conducted in late May, draws on nearly a half-century of research from the General Social Survey, *which has collected data on American attitudes and behaviors at least every other year since 1972. No*

less than 29% of Americans have ever called themselves very happy in that survey.

With everything that is currently going on in our world, it should come as no surprise that people are unhappy, and, as a result, they are definitely pessimistic about the future. But is this pessimism really warranted? Are there reasons for optimism?

I mentioned previously that I consider myself to be an irrepressible optimist with a passion for the impossible who is currently extremely happy with his life. As a matter of fact, I can honestly say I am happier now in this very moment than I've ever been in my life.

Some of you may be wondering how I got here and why am I so optimistic, so this chapter is about sharing the lessons I've learned that have allowed me to become genuinely happy with my life and extremely optimistic about the future.

My journey to happiness began after my divorce. During the darkest period of my life I received a miracle. I was sitting up late one night because I was too depressed to sleep and I was sitting at the foot of my bed staring at my bookshelf across the room. As I sat there staring at the books, I happened to notice that every book on my bookshelf had something to do with getting rich or making money. All of a sudden, I had an epiphany. While sitting there staring at the books, a question just popped into my mind. It came from a voiceless voice inside my head and this was the question I was asked: "Michael, what if you took all of the energy and effort you've used in trying to get rich and used that same energy and effort to learn how to be happy?"

As simplistic as that question may sound, something in me shifted and all of a sudden my depression lifted and I had this amazing clarity that I was going to be able to rebuild my life and it was going to become extraordinary. As a result of asking myself that very question, I stopped reading books on getting rich and making money and I began to read books on philosophy, psychology, metaphysics, quantum physics, spirituality, and personal development. I began what I'll call my journey of transformation and it was this transformational journey that changed my life forever.

Chapter 1: Being Human

At the beginning of my journey, I began journaling as a tool to help me deal with my depression, and while journaling, I came up with a poem that fully expressed how I was feeling at that particular time in my life. I'd like to share the poem with you because there is a deep truth embedded in its message that I'm sure you will be able to relate to.

Here it is:

The Rollercoaster

I had heard a lot about the rollercoaster. Initially I didn't want to go and see it, but everyone kept saying, "You have to check it out and get on it. It will be so much fun."

Reluctantly, I went to see it. It was intriguing and enticing and it looked like fun.

"You have to get on it!" everyone said.

"I'm not sure that I want to."

"But everyone loves getting on the rollercoaster," they said.

"I don't think I'll like it."

"Go ahead and try it, you'll like it," everyone said.

So I tried it.

At the beginning it was fun. Going around and around and up and down with friends who also seemed to be having fun was initially enjoyable.

But after a short while, I got bored and tired. I didn't want to ride it anymore. I decided that I wanted to get off.

"You can't get off," everyone said.

"But I'm ready to."

"No one gets off the rollercoaster once they get on."

"Why not?"

"They just don't.

"But I'm ready to get off."

"Why not ride it a little longer and see if you'll change your mind?" they said.

"Okay, I'll try it a little longer."

Round and round, up and down I went pretending that I was enjoying myself.

But after a while I began to get angry. I was tired of the rollercoaster and I realized that I shouldn't have got on it in the first place. I wanted to get off, but I didn't know how.

"I'm really sick of this rollercoaster. I want to get off right now."

"We're sorry, but you must stay on the rollercoaster. That's the rule."

"Well, I guess I'm going to have to break the rule because I'm about to get off."

"But if you break the rule no one will like you and you will probably get hurt," they said.

"I don't care about anyone else. I want to get off now. Who can I talk to about getting off this thing?"

"No one knows how to get off," they said.

"I'm sure someone knows, I just have to find them."

"It's been said that only a few people have ever got off this rollercoaster. And no one really knows what happened to them. Some believe that people have even been killed trying to get off. Why take that risk?"

"At this point I'm willing to take that risk. I don't care what people think or what people are going to say. I refuse to keep going around and around and getting nowhere on this thing, and I must do something to get off."

I didn't know what to do, but I knew I couldn't stay on the rollercoaster any longer. I needed a plan and I needed it soon. I felt as though I was dying and I really wanted to live again.

But what about the risk? What if what they say is true? What if I really can't get off or what if I get killed trying to get off?

At this point I decided that I had only one choice. And that choice was to live. I didn't know what was going to happen, but I knew if I stayed on this thing I was already dead. I had to trust my inner instincts and take the chance and simply jump off. I wasn't sure where I'd land or if I'd get hurt or even die, but I just knew I had to jump.

Despite what everyone else was saying, and the fear and uncertainty I felt, I took a deep breath and jumped. As my body was hurled through the air uncontrollably, surprisingly I felt a deep sense of calm and inner peace, and then I did exactly what I intuitively knew I could do—I flew!

This poem serves as a metaphor for how we can become trapped by societal and cultural conditioning. As I reflected over the course my life had taken, I realized I had been trapped on this societal rollercoaster and I was doing everything society said I was supposed to do to be happy, but the truth was I was absolutely miserable. I thought by having the house, the wife, the 2.5 kids, the vacations, and the material things, I would be happy, but after "having it all" my life felt empty and meaningless.

In order for you to become genuinely happy with your life you must be willing to jump off of the rollercoaster. This can be scary and frightening, but it is the only way you'll ever truly find happiness. Rest assured if I can do it so can you.

So, are you ready to jump? Of course you are, so let's get started.

There is a quote by Dr. Wayne Dyer that says: "You are not a human being having a spiritual experience, you are a spiritual being having a human experience." If you can embrace this idea you should also embrace that there is a part of you that is divine. That divine part of you is your spirit or, as some might call it, your Soul. Your Soul is your connection to Divine Intelligence. If you're going to jump off of the rollercoaster you're going to have to learn to listen to your Soul. Your Soul is where your courage comes from. It is that part of you that knows deep down inside what you're capable of. Learning to listen to and trust your Soul is the key to finding your purpose and creating a meaningful and fulfilling life.

You're probably wondering how to find and connect with your Soul so that is a great place for me to begin.

In order to find and connect with your Soul it is absolutely imperative that you become willing to make peace with your past and heal any emotional trauma you may have experienced. There are some people who believe it isn't necessary for a person to "dig up old wounds", but I do not hold this view. Based on my own experience, I believe healing emotional wounds is the key to your freedom and connecting to your Soul.

Let me explain why I believe this.

When I began my transformational journey, I was a highly motivated, extroverted, positive thinker who believed science could answer all of my questions about life and this amazing Universe we live in. I was attending a wide variety of personal development type workshops and for the most part I was pretty happy with my life. But after a few years, something was still missing that I just couldn't put my finger on.

During this time I was out of work and living with a friend of mine while I was looking for a job. This friend and I had met at a personal development workshop and we immediately hit it off and became very close friends. It was purely a plutonic friendship that continues to this day almost 25 years later. She and I would have these amazing intellectually stimulating conversations about every imaginable topic and she was the type of friend I would trust with my life.

One evening, my friend came home and asked me how my day went. I told her about the rejections I had received while trying to find a job, and I told her that I was still optimistic that I would find a job soon.

She then looked at me with a caring, compassionate heart and asked how I was really doing. The conversation went something like this:

Her: *Michael, tell me how you're really doing. How are you feeling right now?*

Chapter 1: Being Human

Me: I'm doing great! Although I didn't find a job I'm confident that I will soon and I will be able to get back on my feet.

Her: But Michael, you didn't answer my question. How are you feeling right now? In this very moment how do you feel?

Me: I told you, I'm doing great. I know the Universe is going to support me and help me find a job so I'm excited and happy about my future.

Her: Michael, I think that's bullshit! You keep saying you're doing great but the truth is you aren't. Right now your life is a mess and you're unwilling to be completely honest with yourself about how you really feel. I believe in you and have faith in you that you will get your life on track, but until you are able to be completely honest with yourself about how you feel, not what you think, you really won't be able to change. I personally think that you are in denial and you are hiding behind your positive thinking and denying how you really feel. Can you tell me right now exactly what you're feeling?

Me: I told you, I'm doing great. I've got some challenges to deal with, but I keep telling you I'll deal with them. What more do you want me to say?

Her: I want you to share your feelings with me. Tell me what's going on inside you. Not what's in your head, but what's in your heart. How do you feel?

Me: I don't really understand what you're asking. I keep telling you that I'm fine. What else can I say?

Her: So Michael, answer this question; how does it make you feel not to be able to have your own home and have to rely on other people? Does it make you sad? Does it make you angry?

How did you feel when you were rejected for the jobs you applied for today? Were you upset? Were you disappointed? Were you afraid?

Or how does it make you feel when you know you can't see your kids because you don't have transportation or money to visit them? Doesn't that make you feel sad?

Do you see what I mean now? I want you to share your emotions with me. I want you to express your feelings. Can you do that?

Me: I'm not sure.

Her: Michael, you and I have been through a lot together as friends. I love how you are able to be optimistic and positive, and I love how you can find the good in all situations. But the truth is you aren't connected to your emotions and you hide behind being positive and intellectual. You are so stuck in your head that you can't feel from your heart.

You are my friend and I love you. I will never judge you or reject you. I'm not asking anything from you except your willingness to be authentic and real with me. Can you do that? Can you share yourself with me in that way?

After listening to her for a moment I started to allow myself to feel. I really started looking closer at myself for what emotions were present, and all of a sudden I knew what she meant. In that moment I felt my heart beginning to surrender and I began to speak.

Me: I understand what you mean now. If I'm completely honest I feel sad and afraid. I'm sad because I feel like less than a man because I have to rely on you to take care of me. I feel afraid that I'm not going to be able to find a job and ultimately you will have to kick me out on the streets and I'm not sure what I will do.

Her: That's what I'm talking about. Keep sharing. Tell me more about how you feel.

Me: I really feel like a failure right now. I worked so hard to build my perfect life, only to have it come crashing down on me. I've lost everything. I lost my wife, my kids, my home, my job, and my self-esteem. I feel lonely and sad right now.

All of a sudden my friend walked over and began to hug me. She took me in her arms and told me that everything was going to be okay. She assured me that it was okay to share what I was feeling and that it did not make me less of a man to do so. As she continued to hold me in her warm embrace, I continued to share how I was feeling. I allowed all the trapped emotions to come out and the tears began to flow. I found myself releasing years of repressed pain, sadness, and disappointment, and the emotions just began to pour out of me through my tears. Although it was extremely painful, it was also therapeutic. Allowing myself to feel and express those emotions was extremely healing and cathartic. Before long, my tears of sadness and pain turned to tears of joy as I recognized just how much my friend cared about me and how much love I was feeling from her in that moment.

Me: I am so glad we are having this conversation because I'm really tired of pretending that everything is okay. I have been hiding behind this New Age spiritual positive thinking mask for so long I haven't allowed myself just to feel my emotions. I guess there was a part of me that believed if I shared the negative things in my life it meant I didn't have faith that it would get better. But now I realize this isn't true. Just because I may be feeling sad or afraid does not mean that I've lost faith; it just means that I'm human and I have feelings and I should always be aware of, and true to, those feelings.

Her: The key to happiness is being in touch with how you truly feel and being able to express whatever you feel openly and honestly. Feelings are neither good nor bad, they just are. Emotions are just energy in motion, which really is a human being's way of receiving internal feedback and then expressing your internal response to external stimuli. In reality, our emotions are our internal guidance system that keeps us in touch with our humanness.

Now that we've had this conversation, I hope that you will be able to speak with me openly and honestly about how you really feel, and you should know that negativity isn't necessarily a bad thing. If you focus on it too much it can make matters worse, but the key is to always be honest with how you really feel, no matter what situation you may be in. I accept you unconditionally as a friend and I'm going to be here for you even when things are tough. You don't have to impress me with your optimism and intellect because I accept you for who you are, not what you do. Do you understand?

Me: I really do. This experience has really been good for me and it has opened my eyes to the fact that I still have some healing and some growing to do. Thank you so much for seeing through my positive mask and challenging me to take it off. I promise that I will do my best to be as open and as honest as I possibly can when I'm speaking with you. Thank you so much for being my friend. I love you!

After that conversation I had to carry out some deep soul searching to figure out exactly why it was so difficult for me to initially express my feelings to my friend. As I contemplated our conversation I was able to see a pattern in my life that I had been using for a very long time. I always used positivity as a way of not expressing my true feelings to others, and I always sought other people's approval to feel good about myself.

I knew I wanted to break this pattern, and I decided that I would figure out what steps I needed to take to do so.

I decided to talk to my friend to see if she could begin shedding some light on my behavior. She informed me that one of the reasons why I may have had so much difficulty expressing my feelings could have been the result of some childhood trauma. She shared her own experience about going to therapy to deal with some issues from her childhood, and she suggested that I consider therapy that may help me deal with my issues.

She then said something that really stood out for me. It was a statement that was so powerful it literally caused me to rethink everything I had learned in the personal development arena. She looked at me and said, "I don't care how positive you are, how many books you read, or how many seminars you go to. Until you make peace with your past you will never truly be happy."

It was this statement that challenged me to thoroughly examine my entire philosophy on personal development.

I then realized that all the motivational seminars and books I had read did not help me make peace with my past, so I decided to make it the number one priority in my life. I intuitively knew that making peace with my past was the missing link to finding true happiness.

I ran across a quote by author and spiritual teacher Iyanla Vanzant that fully embodies why making peace with your past is so important. This powerful quote holds the key to your happiness and I suggest that you read it slowly (and several times) and intently so that you fully grasp the implications of its message.

"Until you heal the wounds of your past, you are going to bleed.

You can bandage the bleeding with food, with alcohol, with drugs, with work, with cigarettes, with sex; but eventually, it will all ooze through and stain your life. You must find the strength to open the wounds, stick your hands inside, pull out the core of the pain that is holding you in your past, the memories, and make peace with them."

Herein lies the key to your happiness. What I've learned over the last twenty years is that we must be willing to heal our hearts and make peace with our past if we truly want to be happy. We can read all the self-help books in the world and listen to audio programs or go to seminars with motivational speakers, but if we fail to carry out our healing work we will unconsciously sabotage our lives and ultimately keep ourselves from being completely happy.

After the conversation with my friend, I was reading a book titled *Creating Love* by a guy named John Bradshaw and he was talking about emotional healing. In the book he mentioned that the key to emotional healing was to be willing to create an interpersonal bridge with another human being. What he meant by that was to be willing to be completely open and vulnerable and share the deepest, darkest secrets we may have been hiding from for years. By being willing to share those parts of ourselves that caused us to feel shame, embarrassed, fearful, sad or angry we could heal any of those negative feelings by being willing to share them face-toface with another human being.

As I read that book, I realized this was something that I truly needed to learn how to do. As a result, I decided to participate in a three-day workshop John Bradshaw put on called Healing Your Inner Child.

During the workshop I learned how my traumatic childhood was still having an impact on my life as an adult. My childhood trauma was the reason I was so uncomfortable talking about my feelings. As a result of the trauma, I had actually disconnected from my feelings as a way of dealing with all of the pain I experienced as a child. By participating in this workshop, I was able to heal most of my childhood trauma and reconnect to my emotions. Of course the workshop was extremely difficult and painful. I had to be willing to relive a lot of my childhood pain. But as the saying goes, "If you can feel it, you can heal it." I allowed myself to feel the pain and then move through it with the help of John Bradshaw and some very skilled facilitators in the workshop.

After the workshop my life changed for the better. For the first time in a very long time I became emotionally free. I learned how to feel my emotions authentically and express them appropriately and I also learned that feelings are the language of the Soul, so by healing my heart and learning to feel them I could use my feelings to help me navigate through life.

I could never describe in words the joy I feel as a result of doing that healing work. The best way I can describe it is to say that I am authentically and genuinely happy with myself and I experience a deep level of self-love that is beyond description. I no longer hide behind the mask of Mr. Nice Guy who had an insatiable need for other people's approval, I am now just happy to be me and I need nothing outside of myself to feel loved or appreciated. This is freedom! Freedom to be who I am without any need for external approval.

The interesting thing about motivation is, in most cases, it is temporary. As I mentioned, I was always motivated, yet there was a part of me that knew something was missing. On the other hand, true transformation is permanent. You become transformed and nothing you do can revert you back to your old way of being. Transformation occurs in the heart while motivation occurs in the mind. You can think a certain way, which causes you to act a certain way, but when you no longer think that way the motivation is gone. When you do your inner healing work, you will never go back to the old way of being because you will have changed your heart and that type of change is permanent.

Of course all human beings are different and people deal with trauma in different ways. I share my story because it is how I was able to heal my childhood trauma, but there is a chance that you did not have the same type of traumatic experience as a child. But as a human being, I can assure you that there are probably some unresolved emotional issues that you may have been avoiding in your own life so you must be willing to do some soul searching to find out whether or not you might need to do some emotional healing work.

There are a wide variety of options for you to consider if you are interested in doing some emotional healing. A great place to start might be with a therapist. Of course there is a lot of negative stigma about therapy so I want to ensure you that choosing to see a therapist is not a sign of weakness, it is definitely a sign of strength. There is no shame in saying, "I need help," and right now I would like to give you permission to do so.

My transformational journey actually began with my willingness to go to therapy to deal with depression after my divorce. It was the springboard of my inner journey and it turned out to be a life-changing decision that helped me tremendously.

I would like to share an article I wrote a while ago that shares my first experience with therapy. My hope is that it will give you some insight into how difficult and challenging it might be but also inspire you to take the first step if you think you will benefit from therapy.

The article is titled "Men's Emotional Healing."

In 1989, I had a series of traumatic experiences that were beginning to take their toll. My divorce and separation from my kids were extremely painful and had begun to negatively impact my life. I had slipped into a deep state of depression and was barely able to function on a daily basis. As my depression deepened I went into isolation, where I literally shut myself off from the outside world.

Although I was able to go to work and function in that capacity, I was completely disconnected from any social settings. I was not dating, and I did not socialize with my friends. I also had difficulty sleeping. I would rarely eat and I had begun to lose weight, which was rare for me, being a former personal trainer who took excellent care of my physical body. After several months I began to have fleeting thoughts of suicide, and it appeared that my situation was hopeless. In an effort to alleviate some of the pain, I begin to read books that dealt with depression.

As I read them I could see myself in some of the stories. I definitely had all of the symptoms of depression, and I knew I had to deal with it head-on if I ever wanted to get my life back on track. After reading several books I realized that I was still deeply depressed and had not really begun to deal with the issues that were causing my depression.

Instinctively I knew that I needed help, and I decided that I would seek therapy.

After making the decision to get help, another series of challenges surfaced. First of all, how was I going to find a therapist? How would I know which one to choose? What if the therapist couldn't help me? Would I be able to change? Could therapy "fix" me? What about the money to pay for it? I was completely broke and definitely couldn't pay someone to listen to my problems. What was I going to do? These were just a few of the questions that were going through my mind.

My greatest fear was wondering what would happen if my employees found out. As a manager, I was considered the leader and I definitely didn't want to appear weak in front of my co-workers. I believed that I needed to keep this a secret so that I would not lose the respect of my employees. In addition, I did not want my superiors to know because I thought I might lose my job if they found out.

After a few months of agonizing over these questions I knew I had to take the chance and try therapy. I didn't have any other choice. It was seek help or die—there was no gray area. I decided that I definitely wanted to live, and I somehow gained the courage to seek a therapist.

My first attempt at therapy did not go well. I walked into the therapist's office and pretended that I was seeking information for a friend. I'm sure the people there knew this was a lie, but they allowed me to walk out with some of their brochures and a phone number for their suicide hotline.

To be honest, I was absolutely terrified. But although I was scared, deep down I knew I would have to gain the courage to try again. I waited a few days and tried a different therapist's office. This time I had a completely different result.

As I walked into the office I believe the receptionist picked up on my fear. I began asking her questions about depression and whether or not they had any books that I could read. All of a sudden a therapist walked out and began asking me questions.

"May I help you?" she asked.

"Not really, I'm just looking for a little information about depression."

"Are you depressed?"

"I'm not really sure," I answered.

"Why don't you come inside and let's talk a little. Is that alright?"

"I guess so."

As I followed her into her office it felt as if my heart was going to jump out of my chest. I was so nervous and afraid that I was literally dripping with sweat. She obviously picked up on this and began to put my mind at ease.

"What is your name?"

"Michael."

"Well, Michael, I can sense that you are a little nervous, so let me start by asking what I can do to help you. Is there anything I can do for you?"

"Well, maybe. I have been doing some research about depression and I think I'm depressed, but I'm really not sure."

"Do you feel depressed?"

"Based on what I've read so far I think I am. But to be completely honest I'm not sure I know exactly what depression is supposed to feel like. Does that make any sense to you?"

"It makes a lot of sense to me. Unfortunately most men do not recognize how they feel. Men have been conditioned to disconnect from their emotions and that makes it extremely difficult for them to express how they really feel. Most men will tell you what they think, but they usually do not know how they feel. You apparently fit into this category."

"I'm not sure if I really understand what you're saying, but a part of me thinks that you're right."

"You just validated the point I made. You are currently speaking from an intellectual perspective instead of an emotional one. It sounds as if you are disconnected from your emotions."

"Let's assume that you're right. If I am disconnected from my emotions, how do I get reconnected? Do you have any books on how to do this?"

"Unfortunately you cannot reconnect to your emotions by reading books. In order for you to reconnect you have to relearn how to feel. This can be accomplished through therapy with me or any trained therapist."

"I really don't understand what you mean. But if I decide to relearn how to feel how long will it take?"

"I really can't answer that question. It's really up to you and how committed you are to doing the work."

"What do you mean doing the work? What kind of work is involved?"

"In the therapeutic community we use the word 'work' because it takes a considerable amount of effort to heal yourself so that you can reconnect with your emotions. Doing the work means that you become willing to open yourself up on an emotional level. This can be quite difficult at times."

"Well, I believe I'm ready. I'm really tired of being alone and I definitely want to experience some fun in my life again. I think I can do this, so how much will it cost?"

"I operate on a sliding scale based on your ability to pay. The most important thing is for you to make the commitment to yourself to heal and we can address the money issue at a later date. Are you ready to begin? Let's set up a date and time for you to begin your healing."

"I just want to thank you for being so nice and understanding. The truth is I was about to run out of your office before you showed up. Now I am really glad that I came because I really believe that you can help me."

"That is a great attitude to have. I'm glad that you trust me enough to work with you. Just remember that I can guide you, but you must be willing to do the work. As long as you believe that you can heal I can assure you that you will. Just stay committed and trust the process and you will be just fine. The truth is you have already done the hard part by showing up today. It takes an incredible amount of courage to be here and I'm proud of you for taking the first step."

As I left the therapist's office that day I knew I had just taken the biggest step of my life. I didn't know what to expect, but I knew I was willing to do whatever it took to heal my emotions and relearn how to feel. I became committed to my own healing, and I can now say that I'm emotionally healed and connected to my authentic self.

As the therapist mentioned, it wasn't easy, but it was definitely possible. It has been one of the most challenging, yet most fulfilling, journeys of my life.

I cannot put into words the joy I feel on a regular basis as a result of carrying out my emotional work. My relationships now work, my creativity and sense of reverence is enhanced, my love of nature has been rekindled, and my professional life is rewarding and fulfilling. I took the road less traveled and it has made all the difference in the world for me.

I wanted to share this story because there is such a negative stigma about men and therapy that I believe it's time for a new conversation. In this new conversation men will recognize the importance of healing their emotions and they will put forth the effort to do their healing work.

When we learn to support each other in our growth, we can remove the fear and stigma of being emotionally vulnerable, which will ultimately result in us being happier human beings. I personally believe that this is the most important work men can participate in, and we must begin supporting each other through this process.

If we gain the courage to do this work, we will see a decline in domestic violence, child abuse, alcoholism, and random acts of violence. The time has come for a new conversation about our emotional healing.

Are you willing to join in the conversation?

I am absolutely convinced that the key to your happiness lies in your willingness to do your emotional healing work. By healing your heart and making peace with your past you will then be ready to go a little deeper to connect with your Soul.

I'd like you to read this quote from Dr. Richard Bartlett:

"You are more than your thoughts, your body, or your feelings. You are a swirling vortex of limitless potential who is here to shake things up and create something new that the Universe has never seen."

As you read the quote, what thoughts came to mind? How did you feel after reading it? Did you feel excited? Scared? Confused? Uncertain? What if the quote is true? What if I told you that you are an unlimited being with infinite potential?

Would you believe me?

Unfortunately, most people wouldn't. But the fact that you are reading this book right now tells me that you are not "most people". If you are the type of person who reads a book like this, that tells me that you are open-minded, curious, and willing to learn and grow, and therefore it's quite possible that you believe the quote. As a matter of fact, you've probably already agreed with it and are now ready to create something new that the Universe has never seen—so let's just jump right in and get started.

The truth is there's an overwhelming majority of people who do not believe the quote. They will accept societally driven labels that define who they are without ever asking themselves deeper questions like, "Who am I and why am I here?" This chapter is designed to give you some insights that will possible answer those two questions for you. Are you ready to answer those questions for yourself?

If you ask most people who they are, they will usually respond with answers such as their name, whether they have a family, what they do for a living, if they are a democrat or republican, an African American or Caucasian, a Christian or a Muslim (or are part of a host of other religions), an American or Asian—the list of labels goes on and on. But if you think really deeply about this, these are just titles and labels that we use to try to define who we are. To prove my point, I want you to do a simple test. Walk up to a mirror and ask yourself what you see. Do you see a republican? A Christian? A husband? A manager?

The answer is that you see a human being. The mirror can't lie, it can only reflect that which is placed in front of it. All the titles and labels that you use to define yourself aren't who you are; they are simply titles, labels, and beliefs that you have accepted to define yourself. For example, have you ever known someone who used to be a republican but then became a democrat? Or someone who was a Christian who then became a Muslim? Or maybe someone who was pro-life but then became pro-choice? If they looked in the mirror as a republican and then became a democrat what would they see in the mirror? They would see a human being, not a label. Labels are really just beliefs. You are not a label. You are a human being with different beliefs, and although your beliefs may change, you will not.

What you see in the mirror is what you truly are, but it goes a lot deeper than that. *What* you are is not necessarily *who* you are.

Let me explain in more detail.

What you are is a human being with flesh and bones. This is an undisputable fact. But *who* you are is the divine being that resides within the flesh and bones. Here is another way to look at it—if I stand in front of a mirror and look at myself, I notice that I'm wearing a shirt. So if I say that is "my" shirt, who owns it? I do—it is "my" shirt. Now, I continue to look into the mirror and notice my body. Who is the "me" that owns the body? If this is "my" body, who am I? I would like to suggest that the "me" that owns the body is actually my spirit or my Soul. Put another way, you are not actually a human being having a spiritual experience—you are a spiritual being having a human experience, and your body is just like the suit of clothes you are wearing.

If you can wrap your mind around this idea then Dr. Bartlett's quote should make more sense to you. The quote said, "You are a swirling vortex of limitless potential who is here to shake things up and create something new that the Universe has never seen," which simply means that you are a divine spiritual being expressing yourself through human form. You have unique gifts and talents that must be shared with the world if you truly want to live a rewarding and fulfilling life.

So what do you think? Do you believe this? Can you accept that you are much more than your physical body? Can you embrace the idea that you are a divine spiritual being with unlimited potential who is here to shake things up?

Since you're still reading this book that means you're ready to dive deep into who you really are! So let's begin with understanding your divine makeup.

You are actually a three-part being, which can be described as body, mind, and spirit. You are a spirit housed in a body that has a mind. Your body is like the clothes you are wearing, and your mind is like a tool that you use to help make conscious decisions and to learn new things. They all work in harmony.

As a spiritual being, you have an infinite capacity for learning and creativity. There are absolutely no limits to the amount of things you can learn and create. You are only limited by your imagination, and even your imagination is unlimited.

So, let's break down the three parts of your being. Let's begin with your mind.

It's important that you understand what your mind is and how it works if you truly want to discover who you really are. I'll begin by saying that the mind and the brain are not really the same thing. Your brain is the organ that serves as the center of your nervous system and is responsible for cognitive thinking and memory. In my opinion, it is the most amazing organ in your body, and it works just like a muscle—the more you use it the stronger it gets.

The mind, however, is separate and distinct from the brain, although they work together. It is almost impossible to truly define the mind. Scientists have been trying to define it in scientific terms for millennia, but unfortunately there has never been a consensus on exactly what the mind is. Rather than try to argue and define it, I will simply share a definition that I truly resonate with, and it is this definition I will use to explain what I believe the mind does and how it works.

The mind is "the element of a person that enables them to be aware of the world and their experiences, to think, and to feel; the faculty of consciousness and thought."

I really like the last part of this definition; *the faculty of consciousness and thought.*

According to Dr. Bruce Lipton, author of the amazing book *The Biology of Belief*, the mind actually has two parts; the conscious mind and the subconscious mind. A great metaphor to explain how it works is an iceberg. If you look at an iceberg in the ocean you will only see a small portion of it above the water, but did you know that in some cases 90% of the iceberg is actually below the surface? This is how the mind works. The top 10% is your conscious mind, and the lower 90% is your subconscious mind. What is really fascinating is that the subconscious mind is actually 1000 times more powerful than the conscious mind when it comes to influencing your behavior.

Dr. Lipton explained it this way:

"When we are born, we are completely conscious of all the external stimuli that we interact with. As children we process primarily through our feelings without judgment or thought about the situation. In other words, we use our hearts, not our minds, to interpret everything around us. Our feelings become the guidepost of our experiences.

"During the first 7-10 years of our lives, our subconscious mind works like a video recorder. It simply records all the external events in our lives, and then it begins associating feelings, memories, and beliefs with those events. As we grow older, we begin to form subconscious beliefs about everything we come into contact with. As we form these beliefs we then begin making assumptions about who we are and how we fit into the world. Our prerecorded tapes become our subconscious beliefs about ourselves, and everything we think and do are then filtered through, and influenced by, these prerecorded tapes."

So take a moment to think about your own childhood, especially between when you were born and when you turned seven. What do you remember? Do you remember growing up in a loving, caring home or was it one filled with violence and dysfunction?

Whether you realize it or not, your childhood has a strong impact on your behavior, even as an adult. If you remember being loved and nurtured as a child, the chances are your subconscious mind is filled with positive beliefs about yourself. In other words, your prerecorded tapes are positive, which in most cases means you will feel good about yourself and have a positive attitude about life. On the other hand, if you remember pain and misery growing up, there is a good chance that your prerecorded tapes about yourself may be negative, which in turn may cause you to create a negative outlook on life. This is the reason emotional healing is so important.

You can look at the subconscious mind as a big memory bank that stores your beliefs, memories, and life experiences. All your thoughts are instantly processed through your subconscious beliefs. Look at it this way—once your subconscious tapes are programmed during your childhood, every thought and action you have as an adult will be based on the programming you experienced growing up.

I'd like to take this time to share an example from my life.

I was separated from my mom at the age of six, where I then created a subconscious belief that the people who love you will always leave you. As an adult that may sound irrational, but as a six-year-old, my mother meant the world to me and having her leave me was devastating and emotionally traumatizing.

As a result of this event, I created a subconscious belief that there was something wrong with me that caused my mother to leave. The primary belief I created was that I was unlovable. In order not to feel the shame and abandonment I experienced when my mother left, I created an unconscious strategy that I thought would keep me from feeling pain and also keep people in my life from leaving.

That strategy was for me to become a super nice guy in hopes of keeping people around that I cared about. By becoming a super nice guy I put other people's emotional and psychological needs ahead of my own, and I was constantly trying to take care of others before taking care of myself. This is called *co-dependence*, and it was the reason I struggled with relationships earlier in my life.

Chapter 1: Being Human

I didn't realize it as I was growing up, but that single event laid the foundation of how I interacted in all of my relationships as an adult. My subconscious beliefs about myself actually sabotaged my relationships.

I would enter into a relationship where I would be the super nice guy. I would do all the right things that a woman would want in a relationship. I was attentive and respectful, and I had no problems showing affection. I had a great sense of humor and definitely believed in monogamy. On the surface I appeared to be the perfect guy, but unfortunately my subconscious beliefs about not being good enough and the deep-seated fear of abandonment kept me from being truly authentic in relationships, which kept me from experiencing true intimacy. No matter how much a woman loved me, that deep-rooted fear I had convinced me that something was wrong with me, which led to the fear that eventually the women in my life would leave.

Based on this subconscious fear, what do you think happened in my relationships? Of course, the women in my life would leave. I created an amazing pattern in all of my relationships, especially after my divorce. I would enter into a relationship and it would last two to three weeks, and then the women would end up saying that they "cared too much" about me to stay in the relationship.

At the time, it made absolutely no sense to me that women would say that. How could you care about someone but at the same time leave them? After some deep self-introspection and emotional healing, I was able to recognize how my subconscious beliefs had been sabotaging my relationships, and I figured out how to break the pattern.

The point I'm trying to make is how powerful the subconscious mind really is. Remember, the subconscious mind is separate and distinct from your brain—it is the faculty of consciousness and thought.

On the other hand, you have your conscious mind, which could be referred to as your "intellect". The conscious mind is where you store information that you have learned through rigorous study and learning. When you go to school and learn facts, you are using your conscious mind. When you calculate and figure out solutions to most problems, you are also using your conscious mind, but remember what

I said about the subconscious mind being 1000 times more powerful than the conscious mind?

Here is an example of how this works.

Imagine that you know someone who has a PhD in astrophysics. This person is obviously extremely intelligent and has a highly-developed conscious mind. But imagine too that this person has difficulty creating healthy relationships. No matter what they do, they always experience difficulty in relationships. Why do you think this is? They are obviously very smart, and yet they can't figure out how to make relationships work. Why is that?

Well, it's actually pretty simple. On a conscious level they can read a book about relationships and explain to you intellectually how relationships work, which uses the conscious mind. But their subconscious is 1000 times more powerful than their conscious mind, so when they enter into a relationship, the subconscious beliefs they have about themselves will always override the conscious mind. No matter how many books they read or how smart they are, if they have deeply rooted negative subconscious beliefs about themselves, they will never be able to create healthy relationships.

This is why it is so important to understand how the mind works. No matter how much we may learn on a conscious level, if we aren't willing to look at our subconscious beliefs, we can never truly change our lives. We each have deeply held subconscious beliefs about a wide variety of things and until we become willing to change these subconscious beliefs, we will not be able to overcome our subconscious conditioning.

Let's take a look at some subconscious beliefs that may be sabotaging your life right now.

Are you currently struggling financially and can't figure out why? Well, there is a very good chance that your subconscious beliefs are actually keeping you from being financially secure. If you grew up hearing that money was the root of all evil or that rich people were stuck up and selfish, you may have subconscious beliefs that keep you from making a lot of money because your subconscious belief might be that money is "bad".

If you're a man and you struggle with relationships, you may have subconscious beliefs that say women only want you for your money or women can't be trusted. This belief will eventually sabotage any new relationship you enter. If you're a woman and struggle with relationships, then it's quite possible that you have subconscious beliefs that say all men are dogs and only want sex. Therefore this belief will keep you from creating true intimacy with men because of your lack of trust. If you happen to be religious, you may have subconscious beliefs that you are a sinner and there is nothing you can do except repent of your sins and hope that God forgives you for being a sinner.

No matter what subconscious beliefs you have, you must understand that it is those subconscious beliefs that are actually the cause of most of the pain, suffering, and lack of experience you have in life. To sum it up, your subconscious beliefs create your reality, so if you aren't happy with any area of your life right now, I can assure you that the main reason is that you have some unconscious belief that is causing you pain and misery.

It is absolutely imperative that you begin examining your deeply held subconscious beliefs if you truly want to change, but rest assured that it *is* possible for you to do so.

Now that you have a deeper understanding of how the subconscious mind works, here's the really good news—when you realize just how powerful the mind really is, you can use it to create anything you want in life.

Have you ever heard this quote: "Whatever the mind can conceive, you can achieve, if you really believe"?

Do you believe it? Is it really possible?

I believe the answer is "yes" and now I would like to share how and why this is possible. So let's go back to the definition I posted earlier: The mind is "the element of a person that enables them to be aware of the world and their experiences, to think, and to feel; the faculty of consciousness and thought."

I would like you to focus on "the faculty of consciousness and thought."

Here is another way to look at it. Try to imagine there is a Divine Intelligence that permeates the Universe. This Intelligence is actually the Source of all things. It is inherent in all things. It is what keeps the planets aligned and what causes a seed to grow into a flower. It is the same intelligence that causes a bone to heal and the earth to orbit the sun.

There are lots of different names for this Source, but the name does not matter. You can call it God, The Creator, Yahweh, Jehovah, Great Spirit, The Universe, or any other name, but what is most important is that you believe and trust that it is available to you (throughout this book I will simply refer to it as Divine Intelligence). As mentioned, you do not have to believe in any particular religion or dogma to have access to it, you must simply open your heart and your mind to the truth that it exists. If you accept this truth, then you must accept that your mind is actually connected to Divine Intelligence. Your mind is like a conduit through which Divine Intelligence flows to you and through you.

Now, you must remember what I said at the beginning. **The mind and the brain are not the same thing.** The brain can only process information that you have provided to it. The brain is not creative—it is not the source of imagination, creativity, or divine ideas. The brain is also not the source of inspiration or insight; these are all functions of the mind, which can also be referred to as the heart or the center of your being.

Author and spiritual teacher Iyanla Vanzant said, "The mind is a powerful, creative energy. Everything we think, do, and feel begins in the mind. For this reason, we have to address the thoughts, beliefs, judgments, learning's, and perceptions that we hold in our minds."

The reason the quote "whatever the mind can conceive you can achieve" is true is because Divine Intelligence is purely creative and it needs you to co-create with it. So when your mind conceives a divine idea from Divine Intelligence, which is all-powerful and limitless, you can accomplish it if you're willing to work hand in hand with Divine Intelligence and put forth a whole lot of effort to bring it to fruition.

One of my favorite spiritual teachers is Deepak Chopra. He shared a very powerful quote that really speaks to this truth. He said, "Inherent in every intention and desire are the mechanics for its fulfillment." Put another way, Divine Intelligence will not give you an idea that you can't accomplish. It knows exactly what you're capable of and will therefore only give you divine ideas that are attainable for you. You wouldn't even have the idea in the first place if you weren't capable of accomplishing it.

As I mentioned previously, the mind is the source of imagination, and therefore it is the key to creating anything you want in life. Let me share a brief story with you to validate my point.

During the darkest period of my life I was deeply depressed and unsure of how I was ever going to get my life back on track. At the time, I had no money, no job, no relationship, no material possessions, and things seemed pretty hopeless. But the one thing I did have was my imagination, and I began to use it to help me change my situation. Despite having absolutely nothing, I began imagining my life getting better. Instead of focusing on all the things I didn't have, I focused my attention on what I did have. I would begin each day counting my blessings for everything that I had, such as my health, my ability to learn, my positive attitude, a few close friends, children who loved me, and the fact that I was even alive.

I began envisioning what my life would be like once I got back on my feet, and I somehow knew that eventually I would. As I continued to focus on the things I did have and on the future that I wanted to create, things slowly started to change for me. Eventually I found a job, then I purchased a car, and finally I was able to get my own apartment. Although this took a couple of years, my point is that I used my imagination to see the things I wanted, and then I worked really hard to get them. It all began in my mind. I had to be willing to use my mind and imagination first before I could create the things I wanted.

As I think back in retrospect I can now see how Divine Intelligence was actually the source of all of the ideas that I used to put my life back together. It was Divine Intelligence that would provide me with ideas on where to look for employment, and that gave me the inspiration to remain positive even when I had nothing. It was The Source that gave me the strength and courage to move through all of my life's challenges without giving up and falling victim to despair. It was The Source that encouraged me and helped me to focus on my ultimate destiny, and it didn't allow me to quit.

Even through those difficult times, I held on to my dreams of one day being a successful entrepreneur, writer, and speaker. I had no evidence that I could do these things, I only had the belief and faith that I could. Belief and faith originate in the mind, and I now recognize that each of these originates from The Source.

And now here I am, some twenty years later, doing exactly what I imagined I would be doing. All because I chose to believe that whatever the mind can conceive, you can achieve.

It's important that you understand I am no different than you are. I am a divine spiritual being with direct access to Divine Intelligence, and so are you. There is nothing you cannot accomplish if you choose to access your divinity, but it is up to you to go a little deeper and figure out what negative subconscious beliefs you may have about yourself and change them. It is your responsibility to learn more about your mind and begin using it to create the life you deserve. This is simply an overview of how your mind works. I want you to accept and understand that your mind is the most important aspect of your humanity. Don't take it for granted. Use it to create the life you were born to live. It is your greatest gift from Divine Intelligence.

So, now let's talk about your body.

It is my belief that the most amazing thing on this planet is the human body. I do not believe that there is anything more miraculous. Although most people take their bodies for granted, I believe it is the greatest gift that The Source provided us with. I mentioned earlier that the body is simply a suit of clothing that your spirit wears, so I must admit that The Source knew exactly what it was doing when it created the human body.

Chapter 1: Being Human

Of course, everyone is aware of their own physical body, but did you know that you also have an emotional or energetic body?

If you accept the fact that you are a spiritual being, then it makes it easier to grasp how the emotional/energetic body works.

Think of it this way:

Imagine that you have an opening in the top of your skull, and there is a pipe that goes from the top of your skull to the bottom of your belly. This pipe flows with energy that comes directly from The Source; this energy is your life force, and it permeates your entire being. When you are born, the pipe is completely open and it allows Source energy to flow through you easily. This energy causes you to feel alive and connected to life. This energy is then converted into feelings, which is the spirit's way of communicating with the body. There are primarily four energies that move throughout the energetic body; joy, anger, sadness, and fear.

As a child, whenever you experienced one of these feelings you acted appropriately and expressed the feeling through an emotion. For example, if you felt sad you would cry; if you felt angry you would scream or lash out; if you felt joy you would smile and laugh; and if you felt fear you would close off or retreat. As long as you expressed the feeling appropriately, then the energetic pipe stayed open and clear and your life force energy continued to flow through you.

As you grow older, your parents or family members begin conditioning you to believe that expressing these feelings is wrong, so what happens is you begin to repress and suppress your feelings, and each time you do you begin to create little energy blocks in the pipe. It's like building up plaque in your arteries. The more you suppress your feelings the more the energetic pipe clogs up, and before you know it the pipe is completely closed and you are cut off from your life force. When this happens you lose your sense of aliveness because the divine flow of energy has been cut off. Once the flow of energy has been cut off and we have been disconnected from The Source, we then learn to process everything through our conscious mind or intellect, and we become very rational and analytical. In other words, we try to rely on our brains instead of our minds and hearts.

The bad news is the energetic body works like the subconscious mind. We may not be aware of it, but our repressed emotions cause us to act out irrationally sometimes because we are completely unconscious of the pain we may be carrying. Here is a good example. Have you ever met someone or known someone who is always angry? No matter what is going on, this person is angry and negative and they usually aren't that pleasant to be around. They get angry and upset at the slightest provocation, and no matter what you say or do they will have a negative response to just about everything. Do you know anyone like that? Are *you* like that?

Why do you think this person acts this way? It's because they have trapped emotional energy in their emotional body, and until they learn how to release it, they will always act out of anger.

On the flip side of that, maybe you know someone who always pretends to be happy. They are the "people pleasing" types that always seek approval and they pretend that everything is always okay. The only emotion they express is happiness, but unfortunately they are completely sad and emotionally bankrupt inside. A person like this usually has trapped anger, fear, or sadness in their emotional bodies, and rather than feel these emotions they hide behind being happy all of the time.

When we have repressed or suppressed emotions, they can sabotage all areas of our lives. As long as we feel and release our feelings appropriately, the life force can move through us, but as we shut down the flow, we create a disconnection from The Source and it leads to all sorts of problems in our lives.

It's important that you take care of both of your bodies—your physical body and your emotional one. You take care of the physical body by eating the right foods and exercising, and you take care of the emotional body by investing in some emotional healing work that allows you to release any repressed energy that is trapped in your emotional body. I will share some tips on how to do this in the next chapter.

Now that you have a better understanding of how the mind and the body works together, it's time to fully understand who you really are.

Every major religion promotes a very simple and profound truth; there is a Source through which all things are created. It does not matter which religion you follow as long as you accept this simple fact. This Source is the Divine Intelligence that created and is still creating the Universe, and you have unlimited access to this Source. As a human being you are a divine expression of this Source, which means that you can co-create anything your heart desires with this Source.

Think of it this way—if you look at the ocean, you will see a powerful, beautiful, and seemingly infinite body of water. If you walk up to the ocean and scoop up a small cup of it, what you will have in the cup is ocean. But the cup of ocean could never be the ocean in its totality, so therefore it is a divine expression of the ocean. This expression is no different than the ocean; as a matter of fact it contains all of the same qualities, characteristics, and attributes of the ocean. In fact, it is the ocean in an individualized expression. As long as the expression of the ocean stays connected to the ocean it will thrive and express exactly the way the ocean does. But if the ocean in the cup is separated from the ocean, eventually it will dry up and no longer exist as that unique expression.

The Source is just like the ocean. You are an individual expression of The Source. You have all of the same qualities, characteristics, and attributes as The Source. You are no different than The Source. As long as you stay connected to it you can co-create with it, and since The Source is infinite, so are you.

Do not buy into societal labels and constructs that will convince you that there is something wrong with you. Disregard all labels and titles and come to the understanding that you are a divine spiritual being with unlimited potential, and the only thing that can keep you from accomplishing anything is yourself. This includes letting go of your attachment to your ethnic identity. You should definitely be proud of your ethnic heritage, whatever it may be, but you must understand that your spiritual nature has nothing to do with skin color or nationality.

The Source transcends race, and therefore so do you if you choose to accept who and what you truly are.

Titles and labels will only hold you back, but accepting the truth of your being will definitely set you free. Remember that you are a three-part being—Spirit, Mind, and Body—that is connected to The Source, and you can therefore co-create anything your heart desires.

Once you accept this truth it's important for you to understand the power of beliefs. As you think about the subconscious mind, understand that the subconscious is the storehouse of all your beliefs. Deeply held beliefs are at the core of your life experiences. If your life isn't going the way you'd like it to, rest assured if you change your beliefs your life will change. Your beliefs about a thing actually create your experiences of that thing. Let me share a story to make my point.

There was once a young student who went to a master teacher to learn how to become enlightened. He asked the master what he needed to do to reach his level of mastery and enlightenment. The master teacher took the student to the entrance of their city and set up a small table. As people drove into the city they would approach the master and ask what type of city it was.

After sitting there for a few moments a car pulled up and a couple leaned out of the window and said, "We are thinking about moving to your city. Can you tell us what type of people live here?"

The master smiled and then asked, "What type of people live in your current city?"

The couple replied, "The people from our city are loving, caring, thoughtful, and friendly. We really did not want to move, but our jobs have forced us to."

The master replied, "You're in luck! The people in this city are loving, caring, thoughtful, and friendly. I'm absolutely certain you will be happy here.

"Welcome to our city!"

The couple smiled and drove into the city.

A few moments later, another car pulled up and the couple said,

Chapter 1: Being Human

"We are thinking about moving to your city. Can you tell us what type of people live here?"

To which the master replied, "What type of people live in your current city?"

The couple replied, "The people from our city are cruel, judgmental, backstabbing idiots. We couldn't wait to get out of our city."

The master replied, "I'm sorry to inform you, but the people here are cruel, judgmental, backstabbing idiots also."

The couple growled a bit and drove off.

The student looked at the master with confusion and asked, "Master, why did you lie to the second couple? You told the first couple that the people in the city are loving, caring, thoughtful, and friendly. I don't understand."

The master teacher then said, "Here is your first lesson to become enlightened. I did not lie to the second couple. Your beliefs about a thing will always create your experience of that thing. The first couple believed most people were loving, caring, thoughtful, and friendly; therefore, you can rest assured those would be the type of people they would encounter. The second couple believed most people were cruel, judgmental, backstabbing idiots and I can assure you those would be the type of people they would encounter. A true master knows beliefs are extremely powerful and they actually create your reality. To become a master, you must be willing to change any beliefs that do not support you in reaching enlightenment. It begins with the understanding that our beliefs about a thing create our experience of that thing."

I am a firm believer that your beliefs create your reality and the outcomes of your life.

Have you ever heard of the Bannister Effect?

Before 1954, experts believed it was physically impossible for a human being to run a mile in less than four minutes. Scientists and doctors believed the human body could not withstand that type of stress. But there was a guy named Roger Bannister who didn't believe what the experts said. Roger was a distance runner and neurologist and he believed he could be the first human being to run a mile in less than four minutes.

On May 6th 1954, Roger proved the experts wrong by running a mile in three minutes and 59.4 seconds. Without question this was a breakthrough in human potential, but the story doesn't end there. Within only 46 days someone broke Roger's record, and within a year, several runners had also broken the sub four-minute-mile barrier. The current record stands at three minutes and 43.13 seconds and no one knows how long that record will stand.

So what happened?

Roger Bannister created a paradigm shift. By believing he could run a mile in less than four minutes he accomplished his goal, and after other runners saw him do it, they too believed they could do it and they did. By changing their beliefs they shifted their paradigms and they were able to do what the experts said was impossible.

According to a spiritual teacher called Abraham Hicks, a belief is simply a thought that you think over and over again. If you can change your thoughts, you can change your beliefs, and if you can change your beliefs, you can change your life.

Throughout this book I will be referring to the word paradigm often. I define paradigm as "a rigid way of believing, thinking and behaving." If you want to change your life you will have to create new paradigms in all areas of your life.

So, are you willing to create new paradigms in your life? Do you "believe" it's possible for you to do so? I believe it is, so let's move on to the next chapter.

I'd like to close this chapter with a simple quote from Henry Ford:

"Whether you think you can, or think you can't, you will always be right!"

"The Force is what gives a Jedi his power. It's an energy field created by all living things. It surrounds us and penetrates us. It binds the galaxy together."

Obi-Wan Kenobi

CHAPTER 2
Divine Intelligence & Evolution

When I was approximately 10 years old, I remember being forced to go to church by my grandmother. Even at that young age there was a part of me that was confused and even angry at God for having to go to church. I was confused because I couldn't understand why I couldn't see this guy named Jesus that my grandparents always talked about, and I was angry because I had to get dressed up on Sundays and spend the entire day going to church listening to people talk about something I truly didn't understand.

As a teenager, I was even more confused. I had so many questions that no one could answer. For example, if God was so powerful and answered all of our prayers, why did the minister have to always beg for money? Why didn't his god simply provide the money the preacher was praying for? Another question that really bothered me was this; if God was omnipotent and the creator of all things, how in the world did he allow one of his angels to become his adversary with the power to influence God's creations? In other words, why didn't he just get rid of Satan? Or what about this one, since Jesus was the son of God who was sent here to save us from sin, why did he only get talked about in only four chapters of the Bible? Shouldn't there have been more information about him since he was supposed to be God in the flesh? But the most confusing question of all was why would a loving God send the children that he supposedly loved to spend an eternity in hell simply because they did not believe in his son Jesus? I simply could not wrap my mind around this because it didn't make rational sense to me.

And, of course, there was also the hypocrisy of the preacher. It always bothered me to know that the minister of our church was known to have had several extramarital affairs with members of the church and yet the congregation always forgave him by saying the devil made him do it. To me, since the preacher was the representative of God, God had absolutely no credibility because of the actions of his representative.

These were just a few of the unanswered questions I had about God.

As an adult, I made the choice to stop going to church because of some of these unanswered questions. I guess I would have been considered an agnostic because I wasn't sure if I believed God even existed. So for most of my early adult life, I really didn't give the idea of God much thought.

At the age of 23 I was living the American Dream. I had become the youngest manager of a multi-million-dollar building supply center; I was married; I had purchased my first home; my former wife and I had our first child together; I had money in the bank with excellent credit, and I was in excellent health. On the outside it looked as if I had it all together. But within an approximate six-year time span, my American Dream turned into the American nightmare as I experienced divorce, bankruptcy, foreclosure, vehicle repossession, and depression. At one point I was even homeless for two years living out of my car.

Because of all the pain I was in I decided to go back to church to see if I could alleviate some of the pain. Since I was brought up Baptist, I decided that I would attend a Baptist church. I located a church close to where I lived and decided to attend.

In the beginning there were several things I really liked about the church. The minister was young and energetic and for the most part had extremely positive sermons. This was extremely appealing to me because my previous experiences with church were completely the opposite. I always wondered why sermons were so negative and filled with guilt, judgement, sin, and punishment. In too many cases after church I felt disempowered by the message. But this minister was different; his messages were empowering and life-affirming and I enjoyed the fact that his sermons actually made sense and usually shared a lesson and a story that I could apply to my own life.

In the past, I would listen intently to the message within the sermon and it always amazed me when the preacher would give a disjointed, uninspiring sermon, and, in an attempt to motivate the congregation, he would always rely on the story of Jesus arising from the dead to get the congregation riled up and excited even though that story had nothing to do with his sermon.

But what I enjoyed most about the church was fellowship. As a result of my depression I had begun isolating myself from people, so being around people really helped me lift my depression. Therefore, I spent a lot of time at church volunteering and helping out just so I could be around people.

Initially, the interaction with the people at the church helped lift my depression, but eventually the true cause of my depression wasn't being addressed. I decided to go speak with the minister to see if he might be able to help me, but when I met with him to talk about my feelings of hopelessness his only advice was to simply pray about it. I was a little upset and frustrated by his response, but I decided to take his advice and pray about it.

Unfortunately praying didn't help. I read my Bible and prayed and yet my depression resurfaced and once again I began questioning whether or not I truly believed in God.

After several months, all of my original questions about God resurfaced and I decided to try to answer those questions for myself. I then decided to ask the preacher to answer a question that had been haunting me for a very long time. I scheduled a meeting with him and told him how I was struggling with my faith and I needed him to answer a single question for me. I informed him that his answer to my question would determine whether or not I would stay at his church and continue to believe in the Baptist religion.

Here is the hypothetical question I posed to him:

Imagine there are two people born at exactly the same time in two completely different environments. One of them is born in extreme wealth while the other is born in abject poverty. Now imagine the person who is born in poverty goes through life and based on his environment he does what would be construed as "bad" things. He lies and steals and is angry at the world and therefore he actually hurts other people.

On the other hand, the person who was born into wealth does all the "good things" in life. He is kind and loving and treats everyone with dignity and respect. He gives money to the poor and is respected and loved by his peers.

Now imagine they both die at exactly the same moment and wind up at the entrance to heaven. Standing at the entrance is God Almighty and he is standing at a podium looking through his divine book of life. The two men walk up to God to wait on their fate.

So God calls the man who was born in poverty up to the podium. "Welcome to heaven. Let me take a look at your life and see how well you've done. Hmm, it says here you were not a nice person. You didn't abide by my commandments and you caused a lot of pain and heartache while you were on Earth. Despite these transgressions, I am a loving and forgiving God and I have only one question to ask. Do you receive my son Jesus Christ as your lord and savior?

The man looks up at God apologetically and says, "God, I am sorry for my sins and I do accept your son Jesus as my lord and savior and if you will allow me into heaven I will spend the rest of eternity serving you and your son."

God smiles and welcomes him into heaven.

Next, the man who was born with wealth walks up to the podium and it is very obvious he is extremely nervous. God looks into his book of life and says, "It says here that you were a model human being. You followed my 10 commandments and you were loved by your peers.

Chapter 2: Divine Intelligence & Evolution

I will gladly accept you into heaven, but I must first ask you, do you accept my son Jesus as your lord and savior?"

The man looks up at God nervously and says, "Well, God, I have to be completely honest. Unfortunately, I can't do that. First of all, as an Atheist I am surprised to be here because I never believed you existed. Therefore, I would be lying if I said I accepted your son Jesus as my lord and savior.

God frowns just a bit, closes his book of life, and then informs the man that he will have to spend eternity in everlasting torment in a place called hell.

This was the exact hypothetical question I asked the minister and I asked him if this was how his god worked. Without hesitation the minister looked at me and said, "Yes, this is what the Bible teaches us and this is what I believe."

I sat there for a moment in complete disbelief. All of a sudden, years of frustration welled up in me and this was my response. "Are you really serious? You actually believe a loving God would do something like that? I believe that is the most irrational, illogical, and insane thing I've ever heard. I absolutely refuse to believe that a god would do such a thing. As a matter of fact, you have now confirmed what I have believed all along. There is really no such thing as God and I am willing to risk spending eternity in eternal damnation in a fiery hell before I will believe such an idiotic idea. I respect your beliefs, but I can no longer attend your church because with every fiber of my being I do not believe there is such a thing as God."

In that exact moment I became an Atheist and I walked away from the church.

The good news is my lack of faith in God propelled me to rely on science to answer life's big questions. One of the first questions I had to ask was how I could get rid of my depression. I began reading books on depression and psychology and I began to understand how the mind works. My research led me to therapy and I began to understand how some traumatic events from my childhood were at the root cause of my depression. Therapy opened up a whole new world for me as I began to understand the importance of emotional healing and resolving childhood wounds and I was able to completely overcome my depression.

As I began to feel better and make peace with my past, I committed to continue my growth by reading hundreds of books on psychology, philosophy, metaphysics, and personal development. I became fascinated with neuro-linguistic programming and I became a huge fan of motivational speaker Anthony Robbins who offered an experience called the Fire Walk in which a person would walk over hot coals without getting burned by conditioning their minds to believe they could do it. I actually walked across 1000-degree hot coals during a fire walk ceremony.

As my life continued to improve, I participated in several personal development seminars that allowed me to keep my commitment to constant and never-ending improvement. As a result, I became happier and more fulfilled than I ever imagined possible. During this time I was still an Atheist because I concluded that all of life's questions could be answered through science and reasoning and since I had overcome my depression and was extremely happy with my life I had no need to believe in God.

For the next several years my life continued to improve. I was still reading personal development books and going to seminars but, although I was genuinely happy with my life, something was missing that I couldn't quite put my finger on.

Because of all the research I had done and the books I had read, I had become completely open-minded to always questioning my beliefs and perceptions about the world. It was this open-mindedness that challenged me to reconsider my beliefs about God.

One night, I was reading a personal development book and the author mentioned that he was a Buddhist and he talked about how Buddhism had been the source of his inner peace and joy. Being brought up Baptist I was always taught not to investigate any religion other than Christianity because if you did you couldn't get into heaven. Since I didn't believe in God, I was no longer afraid to do so and I decided to do some research about the Buddhist religion.

As I began to study the religion I had an epiphany. My problem wasn't that I didn't believe in God; my problem was I didn't believe what the Baptist religion had taught me about God. As I studied the Buddhist teachings, something in me shifted and for the first time I felt something "spiritual". As a result, I became obsessed with learning about religions.

I then began my journey to find my truth about God and to find something that I truly believed in and could dedicate my life to.

That journey began with Buddhism. During my personal growth journey, I had begun the practice of meditation and it had really had a positive impact on my life. Initially it was a tool I used to relax and quiet my mind and I approached it from a purely scientific perspective. I didn't equate meditation with spirituality at the beginning, but after studying Buddhism, I learned how meditation is a practice that will actually deepen your spirituality.

I began visiting Buddhist temples and learning more about what they believed. I was pleasantly surprised to learn that Buddhism isn't necessarily a religion but more a way of life. They do not preach about a separate divine being, rather they teach more about the practice of being in touch with your own Buddha nature. It is a belief system that challenges you to think for yourself and not adhere to any rigid dogma or doctrine. There is no sin or punishment and no God that you are supposed to fear and appease. It is a teaching of inner peace and serenity and treating all sentient beings with grace and respect.

After my experience with Buddhism, I decided to take a deep dive into the other major religions. I learned that there are more than 2000 religions around the globe, but I chose to focus on the five most common ones. I read books on Buddhism, Hinduism, Judaism, the Muslim faith and Christianity and I even visited their temples and places of worship to learn what they believed and why. After a few years I came to my very first spiritual truth, which became the foundation of what I believed about God. That truth is: "All faiths originate from the same Source and lead to the same place." This is something that I had always believed without even knowing I believed it.

I'm reminded of something I read a long time ago that said, "God

Is Like Coke, It's the Real Thing." If you take a moment and think about this metaphor I believe it will provide you with a profound truth about God. You see some people will drink Coke out of a can while some will drink it out of a bottle. Cans and bottles come in a wide variety of shapes and sizes. Some people will drink lots of it, while others won't ever touch it. But, ultimately, the container you drink it from is just that, it's a container, it's not God. Therefore, a religion is simply a container that holds God. Each container holds the same thing, God, which is the spiritual thirst quencher.

After studying the other major religions, I was then confronted with another question. What about Christianity? Was it possible the things I was taught about Christianity were wrong? I then began learning about the origin of the Bible and how it had been translated at different times and through some of the translations the true meanings of the teachings were lost. I learned there are 66 different books within the Bible and yet there are other texts that were written yet edited out of the final text.

Without question, the greatest revelation I received about the Bible was that it was not written to be taken literally. It was written to be interpreted metaphysically and metaphorically as a guide to help bring you closer to the Creator who inspired it. The stories within the Bible are allegorical and spiritual and they are to be translated through our hearts not our intellects. If you try to study the Bible literally you'll miss the messages embedded in its pages. By listening to your heart and trusting your intuition the Bible serves as the greatest revelation to man of God's existence.

As a former Atheist, I remember how the word God used to turn me off. Even now the word triggers a part of me that used not to believe it existed. So, my intention is not to try to convince you that God exists. My intention is to simply share some lessons I've learned about God that have helped me develop a deep level of intimacy and connection with it as that is the source of my confidence and optimism about the future of humanity.

The first lesson I want to share is my definition of God. I define God as the Divine Energy and Intelligence that created and is still creating this amazing Universe we live in. The word God is simply a three-letter word man came up with to try to comprehend the incomprehensible. If you try to define God, you automatically put limits on God, and since God is Infinite, words could never fully describe it.

With that being said, I see God as more of a what than a who. We tend to personify God as an anthropomorphic being that looks like us and has the same human emotions and judgements as humans. Some religions teach us that God is an angry and judgmental God, which makes my point. If you believe God is this angry bearded man sitting up in heaven taking notes of your life and waiting for you to sin so he can keep you from entering heaven that is a very limited and inaccurate description of God in my opinion.

On the other hand, if you are open-minded enough to see God as the Divine Energy and Intelligence that created and is still creating this amazing Universe we live in you are on the right track. If you can accept that the intelligence in you that causes your heart to beat, your bones to heal, your hair to grow, the stars to shine, and the planets to stay perfectly aligned, then you know God. Rest assured that you have direct access to this intelligence and when you connect with it nothing will be impossible for you.

The next lesson I'd like to share is that a religion is simply a revelation that was inspired by Divine Intelligence to move humanity forward. If you study the religious texts from the five major religions you will learn that they all point to a simple idea. They each teach us that we have access to this Divine Intelligence called God and the Master teachers within each religion came to teach you how to access the divinity within you.

Another lesson I've learned is you do not have to go to a building to find God. Let me make this abundantly clear; there is absolutely nothing wrong with going to a place of worship and communing with God. Churches, synagogues, temples, and mosques are meeting places to fellowship and worship with others and to deepen your connection with the divine. The truth is, you must be willing to find God in your heart and mind and you do not have to go anywhere to do that. If you follow the teachings of Christ, one of his most powerful lessons came when he was asked about the kingdom of heaven and where to find it; he replied, "The kingdom of heaven does not come with your careful observation, nor will people say, 'Here it is or there it is,' because the kingdom of heaven is within you." This divine truth confirms for me that we all have access to this kingdom and it will not be accessed through a building; rather it can only be accessed through our mind and heart. So, if we do not go within, we will always go without entering the kingdom of heaven. We may go to a building and listen to preachers and ministers, but, ultimately, if we do not develop an intimacy and connection with the divine we will never enter into the kingdom of heaven.

Another powerful lesson I learned is God is love. I've heard people say this most of my life, but I never fully understood its meaning until I went on my own spiritual journey of developing a connection with the god of my understanding. Love is the animating force of life. Everything rises and emerges from this divine love. And since God is literally love, the only thing God can do is love. Therefore, if God is love and the only thing love can do is love, that means everything that happens to us is love. This can be difficult to accept so let me share my experience in hopes of clarifying what I believe.

I wholeheartedly believe there is but one presence and one power in the Universe, God, the good, omnipotent. I do not believe there is a negative evil force or energy (or devil) in the Universe. If I accept this idea, then I must accept the idea that if God is good, everything that happens to me is actually good. (This reminds me of the wise words of William Shakespeare when he said, "Nothing is either good or bad until you think it so.") What I have come to know is this is indeed a very true statement.

As I look back over my life and I reflect back over all of the adversity I had to overcome, like child abuse and abandonment, being a high school dropout, my divorce, bankruptcy, foreclosure, depression, and being homeless for two years, I can now see how every event was actually driven by God's love for me. I can see how it was God's love that allowed me to handle those situations without becoming bitter or giving up on my dreams. It was that love that gave me the patience, perseverance, and faith to hold on to a dream for more than 30 years and to now be able to see that dream coming to fruition. Although these events were difficult and extremely painful at the time, I can clearly see how every event actually shaped me into the man I am today, and if I had to do my life all over again I wouldn't change a thing because, if I did, I would change who I am. Of course, I can clearly see this in retrospect, but during the time of experiencing those events it definitely didn't feel like love. But it was because of the unconditional love of God that I awakened the divinity within me and discovered why I was put here on the planet at this particular time.

This is a lesson I learned through experience and it has cemented my faith and belief in Divine Intelligence.

Divine Intelligence operates through Universal Laws and principles and the principle you should take away from my story is the Breakdown Breakthrough Principle. You can see this divine principle all throughout nature if you're willing to look at the world through a spiritual lens. Take a moment and think about planting the seed of The Coast Redwood tree, which is the largest tree in the world. The Coast Redwood tree can reach heights of 379 feet by 26 feet in diameter. The seed of the tree would easily fit on your smallest fingernail and yet it grows to be so massive and majestic. So, think about this for a moment; how does such a tiny seed grow into such a large tree? The answer is the tree is divinely encoded within the DNA of the seed. The intelligence within the seed knows exactly what it is supposed to become and it automatically begins the process of becoming that which it is. At the beginning, the seed goes through a breakdown period. During this period, you do not see the seed or the tree it is destined to become, but this is the most important time of the development of the seed. This is the time in which the tree begins to develop a root structure to keep it firmly in the ground once it breaks the surface. The bigger the root system the larger the tree will become. Once the root system is firmly in place and rooted in the ground it breaks the surface to become all it was destined to be. As the tree breaks ground and begins to grow it will experience a wide variety of breakdowns, but year after year it continues to grow until ultimately it fulfills its destiny to become a Coast Redwood tree.

As I reflect back over my life I can see how all of the adversities I overcame were the breakdown periods I needed to build a strong root system and foundation to grow upon. My Divine Purpose was encoded into my DNA and fortunately I was able to awaken to my purpose as a writer and speaker. Since the only thing God can do is love me, God knew exactly what I needed to go through to become the grandest expression of my divine self so all of the events of my life were perfectly orchestrated to fulfill a divine plan.

Now, I would like you to consider this possibility since you understand how the Breakdown Breakthrough principle works.

What if humanity is currently going through a breakdown period? What if this breakdown is actually preparing humanity for a breakthrough?

It is my fervent belief that this is exactly what is happening. I believe Divine Intelligence knows exactly what it is doing and without question our world is in total breakdown. But remember, breakdown is always followed by breakthrough. As I look at all the anger, hatred and divisiveness our world is experiencing, rather than believing the world is falling apart, I believe it is actually coming together. But how can I believe that when the media keeps showing how awful the world is?

Think of yourself as a seed that has been planted by Divine Intelligence. Your job first and foremost is to become the fullest expression of your divine self. Once you do that, your goal should be to support others in becoming the fullest version of themselves. Now imagine what type of world this could be if everyone were able to become the fullest version of themselves. Imagine if, all of a sudden, we all recognized the oneness of humanity and we understood there is only one race, which is the human race, and we made a concerted effort to heal the planet and create heaven on Earth. Not only do I believe this is possible, I believe it is inevitable! Why do I believe this? Because I believe in Divine Intelligence and I believe it knows exactly what it is doing and we are destined to have a major breakthrough after we move through this temporary breakdown.

There was an amazing woman named Barbara Marx Hubbard (December 22nd 1929 – April 10th, 2019) who wrote an incredible book called *Conscious Evolution*. I have been deeply influenced by her work and I agree with her theory that human beings are actually still evolving and though we may not be evolving physically we are evolving in consciousness. This evolution in consciousness is driven by Divine Intelligence and there is nothing that can stop it. This is my primary reason for optimism about the future.

So, what do you think? Do you think human beings are still evolving? Do you believe there will be a breakthrough after the current breakdown? Or maybe you believe I'm one of those New Age kooks that is out of touch with reality. As I mentioned at the beginning, my job is not to try to convince you to believe what I believe. My job is to provide you with a different perspective about the world and how you fit into it.

So ask yourself honestly, what do you really believe about the current state of our world? What do you believe about Divine Intelligence?

I believe the more important question is are you willing to become the divine seed you were planted to be? Are you willing to become your version of the majestic Coast Redwood tree?

If you're still reading, I am going to assume you are ready to wake up the divine DNA within you so you can fully express who you truly are. To do so, I'd like to share three things you must do to awaken to your divinity.

1. First and foremost you must acknowledge that there is a part of you that is divine. Put another way, there is a part of you that is connected to Divine Intelligence and once you connect to it, you will be able to accomplish anything you set your mind to. You must accept the fact that you were not born a sinner, and no matter what you may have done in your past it doesn't make you a "bad" person. We all make the best possible choices for ourselves, in that moment, based on our limited amount of understanding. Therefore, if we understood better we would have made a better choice. You have made choices in life and you obviously must accept the consequences of those choices and if you are unhappy with the consequences, you must learn

to make better choices, and to make better choices you must increase your understanding. Once you understand that you have access to Divine Intelligence, rest assured you will begin making better choices.

2. You must commit to your own inner transformation. This can be the most difficult part, but rest assured you have everything you need already inside of you to do this. A very wise person once said, "Do not be conformed to this world, but be transformed by the renewing of your mind." Renewing your mind is what inner transformation is all about.

3. Committing to your inner transformation means you must be willing to challenge deeply held beliefs and assumptions about yourself and the world around you. As I mentioned in my story, I had to be willing to challenge my beliefs about God and not accept what I was taught from a very early age. I had to do my own research and investigation and ultimately come to my own conclusions about what I believed about God. In other words, I had to find my own truth. To do this, you must understand that you may have to disappoint others in order to be true to yourself. But ultimately this is your primary goal, to find your truth about God and about yourself. In the next chapter I will be sharing some specific things for you to do to support your personal inner transformation.

4. Lastly, you must come up with a way to serve others. Being in service to humanity is a surefire way to find more meaning and purpose in your life. Muhammad Ali said it best when he stated, "Being in service to others is the rent we pay for our time here on Earth." Serving others simply means you are willing to share your unique gifts and talents with others to make the world a better place. It doesn't necessarily mean you have to impact the lives of thousands of people. It means you are willing to contribute something to the world that makes it a little better. You can volunteer your time at a homeless shelter or food bank; you can become a mentor for youth; you can smile at someone and say a prayer for them or you can

donate money to a family in need. These are all different forms of being in service and in doing so you will also be served. The joy you will receive will be the payment for services rendered and that feeling is worth any effort.

These are three simple steps to accessing your divinity, but remember, simple does not necessarily mean it's going to be easy. But if it doesn't challenge you it can't change you, so remember the Breakdown Breakthrough principle as you embark on this journey.

Your takeaways from this chapter are:

There is a Divine Intelligence that permeates this Universe and you have direct access to this intelligence. This intelligence operates through Universal Laws and principles and the primary principle to remember is the Breakdown Breakthrough principle. Divine Intelligence knows exactly what it's doing and it is expressing itself as evolution. Evolution is the process of moving towards deeper and deeper levels of complexity and human beings are still evolving in consciousness, which will ultimately lead to a unified humanity.

Your purpose in life is to become the grandest version of the greatest vision you have for yourself as a human being. (To quote Neale Donald Walsch) Once you awaken to your divinity, you are committed to doing your part in making the world a better place by being in service to others by sharing your gifts and talents.

But most importantly remember this; life was meant to be good but no one said it was going to be easy. It's up to you to find your joy and be willing to spread it.

I'll close this chapter with a quote from one of my favorite spiritual teachers, Mike Dooley. Mike sends out a daily email called Notes from the Universe and each morning I spend some quiet time in meditation and then I read his messages and contemplate their meaning. Without fail they are humorous, insightful, thought-provoking, transformational and deeply spiritual. Although he is the author, he recognizes that it is Divine Intelligence that inspires his notes. If you are not familiar with his work, I highly recommend that you check him out. It will be well worth your time to connect with him and learn from him. www.tut.com

Here is one of his Notes from the Universe, that really resonates with what I've been writing about in this chapter.

"I know that there's the "you" that you know you are—adventurous, good-looking, and fun to be around.

"And I know you know that there's another part of 'you' in the unseen who you've kind of temporarily forgotten—who completes you, loves you, and knows what's really going on.

"Well, how'd you like it if I removed the veils? Just for a second? Gave you a glimpse of who that special, divine, otherworldly essence is, so that you might at last begin to comprehend how extraordinary, sublime, and divine you really are?

"Okay?

"It's me!

"Yours truly,

"The entire flippin' Universe"

"I define spirituality as the moment to moment recognition and acknowledgement of my connection to something greater than myself."

Coach Michael Taylor

CHAPTER 3
Spirituality

According to a Pew report, more and more people are moving away from organized religion. While some may see this as a move away from morality, I see it as a movement more towards developing an intimate connection with Divine Intelligence. I don't believe most people are moving away from believing in God, they are actually moving towards gaining a deeper understanding and connection to God. Now more than ever, people are identifying with the term "spiritual not religious" and I believe there is a huge distinction to be made between the two.

So, what is the difference?

To fully understand the difference, let's begin by listening to two of the most brilliant men and greatest minds the world has even seen.

Albert Einstein once said, "Everything is energy, that's just the way that it is. Match the frequency of the reality you want to create and there is no way you can't create that reality. It can be no other way. This isn't philosophy, this is physics."

Nikola Tesla said, "If you want to understand the Universe you must think in terms of energy, frequency, and vibration."

Both of these brilliant minds point to a scientific fact. Everything is energy!

So where did this energy come from?

This is the million-dollar question.

To answer it you have three options.

Option 1. It was a random act that just happened.

Option 2. Something caused it to happen.

Option 3. You do not know where it came from.

Option number one is based on science. Science says there was a Big Bang that occurred randomly and the Universe is the result of a chemical reaction that evolved into our current Universe.

Option number two is based on a belief that there was a Creator that caused the Universe to take form. Every religion is based on this option.

Option number three is, "I really do not know!"

So which option best describes what you believe, Option #1, Option #2, or Option #3?

To fully understand the distinction between religion and spirituality let's go back several thousand years. Try to imagine what it must have been like to be a caveman. During that time your primary responsibility was to provide food and shelter for you and your family and to protect you and your family from being eaten alive by dinosaurs. For the most part it was a pretty simple life. You didn't have language, but you learned to communicate with pictures and sounds. As cavemen evolved, they developed language and learned to make weapons and basic tools for their survival. As they continued to evolve they realized there were certain things that they didn't understand or have control over so they came up with stories and ideas to try to make sense of natural phenomena. For example, if lightning would strike they had no idea where the lightning came from so they created stories to try to explain where it originated from. They then came up with the idea that there was some sort of powerful force in the sky that was shooting lightning bolts at them. If they contracted a disease, they created stories that said the gods up in the sky were angry and were punishing them for one reason or another. So, it was man's lack of understanding the physical world around them that caused them to come up with explanations of things they didn't understand. Therefore, these stories became religions.

As these stories were passed down from generation to generation, human beings were still evolving and there were some very evolved beings that began teaching that there was a Creator of all things and they provided some new stories about how this Creator operated. These evolved beings laid the groundwork for all religions and their teachings spread across the globe.

The problem as I see it was each of these evolved beings shared a message of oneness with the Creator; however, each evolved being had their own unique interpretation of what the Creator was expecting from human beings and they shared their "truth" with the masses, and then the masses started sharing those truths with others. Unfortunately, a lot of the messages of the evolved beings got lost in translation and were misinterpreted and even completely changed. Yet, the masses concluded that their evolved being was the chosen evolved being, and if you didn't follow their evolved being's way of worshipping God then you could not be a part of their evolved being's tribe. So, each tribe believed their evolved being was teaching the "right" way to connect with God and the other evolved beings were teaching the "wrong" way of connecting with God.

Therefore, a religion is a belief in a story of an evolved being that came to teach human beings how to connect to the Creator. The downside of religion is they promote exclusivity. If you do not believe in their teachings you are seen as different and separate from that particular group. In other words, if you do not believe in what they believe, you cannot be a part of their tribe. This is the core essence of religion.

On the other hand, you have spirituality. Spirituality suggests there have been several evolved beings that have walked the earth and each one shared the same message. Their primary message is there is a Divine Creator of the Universe and every human being has equal access to this Creator. Being spiritual but not religious means you recognize that all religions originate from the same source and lead to the same place and therefore you accept that some people may believe in a different

God than you but that doesn't mean they can't be a part of your tribe. Spirituality is all-inclusive and welcomes all human beings into one Universal tribe.

There was a time when I believed in option #1. As I mentioned in a previous chapter, I concluded there was no such thing as God and I held firm to the belief that science held the answer to everything and if it couldn't be proved by science it simply wasn't real. But then I made a paradigm shift. I changed my rigid way of thinking by researching the different religions and coming to my own conclusions and beliefs about God.

To provide you with some fuel for contemplation, I'd like to share some things I've learned that confirm for me that science and spirituality actually go together. I realize there are some people who may not believe this, but since you're still reading I am going to assume you are open-minded enough to believe what I am about to share.

Let's go back to the quote, "everything is energy." There is a scientific process called reductionism, which means you can take anything and reduce it down to its smallest component to know exactly what it is made of. There was a time when scientists thought the smallest particle of matter was the atom so they concluded that the atom was the building block of all matter. As science evolved and technology increased they realized the atom wasn't the smallest particle of matter. When they broke down everything into its smallest component, they realized that everything was actually composed of energy. In other words, nothing is actually solid. It's energy vibrating at different speeds and as this energy slows down it becomes solid matter. Dr. Joe Dispenza explained it this way, "If you stripped an atom down to its raw essentials, all that exists is energy & information, but the atom is not without design. Even at that quantum level, there exists a structure and orderliness, so there must be some intelligence or force that is unifying and ordering them."

So what is this intelligence or force and where did it come from?

Once again, this is the million-dollar question. Did this energy and intelligence randomly appear or did "something" cause it to appear?

As a result of my own research I have come to some conclusions on my own that I would like to share with you. To fully grasp what I'm about to share it may require you to create a new paradigm about what you believe about how the Universe began.

I'd like you to try to imagine complete darkness and emptiness. Put another way, try to imagine complete nothingness. In this nothingness, nothing exists. There is no light or darkness or even time. It is pure nothingness. Can you imagine it? Now try to imagine that all of a sudden something came from nothing. If you believe in science, the instant something that came from nothing was called the Big Bang. If you're religious, it was in that moment that God said, "Let there be light." Either way, the point here is at first there was nothing and then there was something. If you choose to see this event through a scientific perspective how would you explain that? If there was absolute nothingness and then something came from nothing, that means the nothingness was actually something because it would be impossible for something to come from nothing. Are you still with me here? Think deeply about that. How could something come from nothing? I would like to propose that that nothingness is actually something, and that something could be called Pure Consciousness or Divine Intelligence, or, if you're religious, you can call it God. As I see it, it is the Source of all things. Everything in the Universe arises from this Divine Intelligence. The instant something came from nothing, an energy was released and there is an intelligence that drives this energy. The intelligence that drives this energy is called evolution. Evolution is the process through which Divine Intelligence evolves to deeper and deeper levels of complexity and this is an ongoing process that will continue throughout eternity.

This energy is within you and true spirituality is developing an intimacy with and connection to this energy. You do not have to be religious to connect to this energy. Even if you do not believe in this energy it is still there. Each religion is supposed to help you recognize this energy within you, but, unfortunately, most religions get caught up in religious dogma and doctrine and fail to teach you the truth of accessing this energy. If you're familiar with Christianity, you may remember what Jesus said about entering the kingdom of heaven. In

Luke 17:20–23 he said, "The kingdom of God does not come with observation; nor will they say, 'See here!' or 'See there!' For indeed, the kingdom of God is within you."

My interpretation of that scripture is Jesus is telling us to look within our own hearts and minds and connect to the Divine Intelligence, which is the energy within us. Therefore, your goal should be to come to your own understanding about God and not just accept what you've been told but research and find your own truth about God so that you can develop an intimate relationship with this Divine Intelligence.

I want to share an excerpt from my book *Adversity Is Your Greatest Ally*. In this excerpt, I'd like to share my story of finding a spiritual home and philosophy that truly resonates with my Soul and is the foundation of my spirituality.

Here is the excerpt:

So, let me ask you a question: What are your beliefs about God?

Notice I didn't ask you if you believe in God, I asked what are your beliefs about God. For some people, they may not believe God exists. For other people they may have a very strong belief in God. Some may believe in an anthropomorphic god sitting in heaven taking notes of their lives and waiting for them to die to see if they are able to get into heaven. Others may believe in a god of love who loves them unconditionally and accepts them with open loving arms and showers them with grace.

If you truly want to know what type of god you believe in let me suggest you simply take a deep look at your life right now and you will find your answer. As I mentioned earlier, your belief about a thing creates your experience of that thing. So, if you believe in an angry, judgmental god to whom you have to repent of your sins to try to get into heaven, chances are your life is filled with fear and anxiety. On the other hand, if you believe in a god of love then your life could be filled with joy, inner peace and happiness.

But ultimately your beliefs about God will always create your experience of God, so it's important to be really clear about what you believe. I am convinced most people really do not know what they believe about God. They may know what they were taught to believe about God through their families and their cultures, but they have never really questioned or challenged those beliefs. They have simply accepted beliefs that may have been passed down for generations and they are absolutely convinced that their beliefs are the "right" beliefs and anyone who doesn't believe what they believe is "wrong".

Once again, my job is to simply share some insights and information that have allowed me to develop an intimate connection to Divine Intelligence and ultimately you get to decide whether or not you believe them or not.

With that being said, I wanted to share a little miracle story about how I found the perfect place for me to develop my spirituality and my connection to Divine Intelligence.

During the early '90s I attended a personal development workshop called LifeSpring. During the workshop, I had a conversation about God with one of the other participants. She asked me if I had ever heard of a church called Unity and I told her no. She then told me that I would love it because it was a positive approach to Christianity and she said I was the most positive person she'd ever met and she knew I would fit right in. She even mentioned they were so positive that sometimes she didn't go because she was actually uncomfortable with so much positivity.

A part of me was a little hesitant, but since I wanted to learn more about Christianity I told her I would eventually check it out.

Here is where the miracle happened.

The very next day, I was at home sitting at my kitchen table looking through a phone book for something. All of a sudden my phone rang so I got up to answer it. When I got up, I accidently knocked the phone book onto the floor. After I completed my call I picked up the phone book and when I laid it on the table and looked inside, there was an advertisement for Unity Church. I smiled because I immediately recognized the synchronicity and jotted down the phone number to give them a call.

It turned out the church was only a few minutes away from where I lived so I knew I was supposed to go. I decided to drive by even though they were closed just to check it out. As I looked through the window of their bookstore I was pleasantly surprised to see books from some of my favorite authors regarding personal growth and spirituality. Now I was really excited and couldn't wait until Sunday.

When Sunday came around, I parked out front and decided to see what type of people would be going in. I knew there would probably not be many black people attending because this was definitely not a traditional church setting. I decided to go in and I experienced another miracle.

There are some events in our lives that change the trajectory we are on forever. Some people would call them transcendent experiences while others might use the word divine. I'm not sure exactly what to call it, but as soon as I stepped into the church something in me shifted. A part of me screamed with joy and delight as if knowing I had found my home. I could never fully explain it in words, but the closest I can come to describing it is by saying I was bathed by a holy spirit. It was a palpable feeling of being touched by something divine. My Soul lit up like a Christmas tree inside.

Once I walked in my suspicions were confirmed. I was the only black person in the church, but it definitely didn't bother me because I was surrounded by nothing but love. I could feel the unconditional non-judgmental feeling of acceptance and it felt wonderful.

The first thing the minister said was, "It's time to begin our service with a meditation." What? Do they meditate in a Christian church? Is this real? I remember telling one of my Christian friends that I had begun meditating and she said meditation was trafficking with the devil. And now there I was in a Christian church meditating. Had I died and gone to heaven? It sure felt that way.

After the meditation, the minister gave a loving and inspiring sermon that opened my heart and filled me with the divine love of God. It was absolutely beautiful.

After the service, I was greeted and acknowledged for coming and of course they extended an invitation for me to join their church. Although I knew I would eventually be joining the church I declined their invitation so I could learn more about it. The experience was so new and different from what I was accustomed to I wanted to make sure I wasn't being pulled into some type of cult or something.

So I grabbed some of their material and went home to learn more.

Chapter 3: Spirituality

During my research, I learned that Unity began in 1889 with Charles and Myrtle Fillmore. It is a nondenominational New Thought Church that teaches a metaphysical interpretation of the Bible that encourages its congregants to recognize that every human being has a spark of divinity within them and Jesus came to teach you how to access that spark.

Although I was impressed with what I learned about the church, it wasn't the material that convinced me to want to join. It was that feeling I received the moment I walked in and it was my own inner wisdom that was guiding me to join.

During that time in my life, I was experiencing a lot of adversity and difficulty and I ended up having to move away from my home in Houston. I actually moved away to live with my brother because I didn't have a job and I had run out of money.

I moved to Austin and the first thing I did was find a Unity church. I started attending services on a regular basis and I committed myself to their teachings. One of their teachings is there is but one presence and one power in the Universe, God the good omnipotent, and therefore if I am experiencing any adversity or challenge it isn't that I'm being punished, I'm simply being redirected to something better. So despite my financial situation I accepted this truth and held firm to the belief that I was being guided to something bigger and better in my life.

Although it was difficult, I held firm to this belief for a couple of years before my life actually started getting better. But those challenges only deepened my faith and ultimately things started turning around and I was able to get back on my feet and move back to Houston.

Once there, I immediately found another Unity church. After years of following their principles, I had developed my faith from just believing in God to knowing there was God. With this newfound faith, I decided it was time to fully commit to the Unity teachings by becoming a member.

But a part of me still had some negative residual effects from joining the Baptist church. I then decided that I would go and speak to the minister before I joined just to remove any doubt that I was doing the right thing.

When I met with the minister, I told him the story about why I had left the Baptist church. I also told him that I really didn't trust preachers but since joining Unity my beliefs had definitely changed. He then said something that would put my mind at ease and confirm I was making the right decision. He smiled at me and said, "The most important thing for you to understand is I am no closer to God than you are. You have the same access to God that I have. My job is to simply help you deepen your connection to God because that is where your inner peace and power will come from. Therefore your relationship isn't with me. Your relationship is directly with God." There was a calmness and sincerity in his words that truly comforted me. Unlike the experience I'd had with the Baptist minister, I had a deep sense of connection and sincerity with this Unity minister. A part of me knew I had found my church home and my Soul was comforted by my decision to join.

From that point on I joined the church and I became truly committed to the Unity teachings. I took several courses and attended lectures to learn all I could about the Universal principles they taught. I even taught Sunday school to teenagers and even considered becoming a Unity minister but then decided against it because I came to the conclusion that I didn't have to be a minister to have a ministry. I then began my ministry by writing books and becoming a speaker who shares the wisdom and lessons I've learned on my own spiritual journey with others. I have now created my version of an extraordinary life and I am happier now than I've ever been in my life. Has it been easy? Of course not! Was it all worth it? Absolutely, unequivocally, yes!

As I reflect back over the past 25 years or so of my spiritual journey I am in awe of the grace and love of God. As I look back I can see how every adversity no matter how difficult or painful brought me a gift and a lesson that was for my highest good. If I had to do my life all over again I wouldn't change a thing because I now see the perfection in all of it. If I changed any part of it I wouldn't be the man I am today.

I mentioned earlier that my intention isn't to try to convince you that God exists. However, I would like to share a couple of truths that have allowed me to develop an intimacy and connection with a power greater than me that allows me to know beyond a shadow of a doubt that God is real. I'm not asking you to believe what I say, but I am asking you to simply contemplate these ideas and see if they resonate with you.

First of all, it's important for you to find your own truth about God. Most people simply accept what has been passed on to them without truly asking themselves what they really believe. So my suggestion for you is to honestly ask yourself what you believe and why you believe it. Be willing and open to the idea that what you may have believed in the past isn't true. Be willing to be wrong about God so ultimately you'll be right about God. In other words, find what's true for you. To do this you will have to challenge some deeply held beliefs, but rest assured when you authentically find your truth it will be worth any discomfort you may have to go through.

Next, always remember there are many paths to God and just because someone is on a different path than you are it doesn't mean they are the ones who are lost. Find your truth and allow others to find theirs. I can assure you if you will find your authentic truth it will not matter what other people believe and you will not feel the need to try to convince others that your truth is the truth. Find your truth!

Last but definitely not least, develop intimacy with and connection to a power greater than yourself. Remember, the name isn't important, but nurturing and creating the connection is. My suggestion is to develop a spiritual practice that keeps you connected to this power and let me recommend that having a meditation practice is one of the best ways to create and maintain that connection.

In closing, my hope is that you have an opportunity to experience the unconditional love of a loving Creator. It is a feeling that is so deep you could never put it into words. It is like feeling the unconditional love of a child or being kissed by the beauty of a sunrise or sunset. It is joy; it is passion; it is reverence and love all rolled up into one thing. It is God and yet that word doesn't come close to expressing what it is. Skip the word and go for the feeling. Ultimately, it's even more than a feeling; it's the reality of the whole world.

I hope you get to feel it!

"A racist is someone who harbors anger and hatred in their hearts towards people of another race because they believe they are superior because of their race. The overwhelming majority of human beings are not racists."

Coach Michael Taylor

CHAPTER 4
Race

In August of 2016, former NFL quarterback Colin Kaepernick began a protest to bring awareness to police brutality and racial inequality in America. His protest began with him sitting during the national anthem, but after speaking with his teammate Nate Boyer, he decided to kneel during the anthem rather than sit. During an interview with NFL Media he said, "I am not going to stand up to show pride in a flag for a country that oppresses Black people and people of color. To me, this is bigger than football and it would be selfish on my part to look the other way. There are bodies in the street and people getting paid leave and getting away with murder."

His protest set off a firestorm of controversy and ignited a much-needed conversation about race in America even though it did evolve into one of the most divisive political issues this country has had to deal with. Despite the fact that Colin insisted his protest was about police brutality and racial equality, the media reframed the protest as disrespecting the flag and the military. Immediately, the protest created racial divisions and he was perceived as unpatriotic. The racial divisiveness really escalated when the president of the United States was speaking with a group of his supporters and said, "Wouldn't you love to see one of these NFL owners, when someone disrespects our flag, to say, 'Get that son of a bitch off the field right now. Out. He's fired. He's fired'?"

On May 25th 2020, George Floyd attempted to purchase some cigarettes with a counterfeit 20-dollar bill from a convenience store in Minneapolis. The police were called and, within seventeen minutes, George Floyd had been pinned down on the ground by Officer Derek Chauvin. A video shows Officer Chauvin with his knee on George's neck for eight minutes and 46 seconds. During that time, George continuously told the officer he couldn't breathe and even after he went unconscious, the officer kept his knee on his neck for a full minute and 20 seconds. Sadly, George Floyd died and the world had front row seats to a white police officer killing a black man on national television.

This tragedy set off a series of protests and propelled the Black Lives Matter movement into the international spotlight. People around the globe joined the protest and, all of a sudden, in some ways, Colin's protest was being vindicated. People around the globe began to recognize what he had been saying from the beginning; his protests had absolutely nothing to do with disrespecting the flag or our military. It had everything thing to do with keeping police officers from killing the George Floyds of the world.

Even now, some six months later, the protests are still going on in different places around the globe and the racial tension can still be felt as a result of George Floyd's murder.

Which leads me to ask this question: Are race relations getting worse in America and around the globe?

At first glance it appears the answer is an emphatic yes. If you pay attention to mainstream media it will be easy to find the evidence to support this idea. In America, we have recently had a president who refuses to denounce white supremacy and is even unwilling to even say Black Lives Matter. We have white women who are calling police officers on black men for no reason and even falsely accusing them of assault. We have a resurgence of white supremacists and hate groups around the globe and the issue of immigration is causing anger and division in countries around the world. So, on the surface, it appears that race relations are definitely getting worse and are definitely heading in the wrong direction.

And yet, I have a different perception and opinion. Although I recognize the current challenges the world has in regards to race relations, I happen to be extremely optimistic about race relations. The primary reason for my optimism is my belief in Divine Intelligence. As I've mentioned before, Divine Intelligence set this entire Universe in motion and it has a specific intention, and I believe that intention is to ultimately create heaven on Earth. This does not mean that the world will become some sort of utopian airy-fairy hippy colony with everyone loving each other and singing kum-ba-ya; it means human beings are evolving to a point where war, poverty and the belief that human beings are different and separate will eventually become things of the past and the world will be able to live in peace and harmony.

As I reflect over the past few months, something feels different. There is a palpable shift in consciousness as a result of the George Floyd incident. Collectively, it feels the same way it felt when Dr. Martin Luther King was assassinated. Although there are definitely feelings of anger, frustration and sadness, there are also feelings of possibilities that something has changed in the minds of the masses. It feels as if the heart of America has been cracked wide open and people are longing for racial reconciliation and togetherness. This is evidenced by the amount of conversations white people are having about race relations.

It is my belief that this country went into a state of denial about racism when Barack Obama became president. It seems like a lot of white people thought racism was over because we had chosen a black president. As a black person I knew otherwise, and I'm certain most black people felt the same way. We realized this country had taken a step in the right direction, but we also knew that there were systemic problems that would not be solved simply by choosing a black president.

As a result of the George Floyd tragedy, I've noticed a shift in conversations with white people. There have been a lot of conversations about white privilege and white fragility and collectively it feels like white people genuinely want to heal the racial tension in our country. Watching the brutality of George's murder opened some eyes to the fact that racism is still alive and well in America and I believe it has generated compassion and empathy for black people in general.

I had a group of primarily white women contact me and ask if I could do an online webinar to talk about the racial challenges we were dealing with and they asked if I would be willing to share some insights from my book *Shattering Black Male Stereotypes*. I have to admit the participants were genuinely interested and engaged with the content of my presentation and each of them were open and receptive to my message. Afterwards, they thanked me for the insights I shared about the challenges of being a black male in America and I believe their minds and their hearts were changed about the unique challenges black men have to deal with on a daily basis.

My belief that we are actually making progress in terms of race relations was also confirmed by a comment made by NFL Commissioner Roger Goodell. When Colin Kaepernick first began his protest, he had absolutely no support from the NFL. As a matter of fact, he was blackballed from the NFL as a result of his protest. Despite the fact that he was at one time one of the best quarterbacks in the NFL who actually led his team to the Super Bowl, he has not been accepted back into the NFL even though he is a much better player than a lot of quarterbacks who are now playing.

In an interview on Emmanuel Acho's critically acclaimed show *Uncomfortable Conversations with a Black Man* (which is an amazing show and another reason for my optimism), Mr. Goodell expressed regret for the league not listening to Colin when he began protesting. This is what he said:

"What our players are doing is being mischaracterized. These are not people who are unpatriotic. They're not disloyal. They're not against our military, what they were trying to do is exercise their right to bring attention to something that needs to get fixed. That misrepresentation of who they were and what they were doing was the thing that really gnawed at me."

Another person in the NFL who changed their mind about the protest was New Orleans Saints quarterback Drew Brees. At the beginning, here is what Drew said about the protest:

"I will never agree with anybody disrespecting the flag of the United States of America or our country. Let me just tell you what I see or what I feel when the national anthem is played and when I look at the flag of the United States."

The quarterback said he envisioned his grandfather's fighting during World War II and risking their lives to protect the country.

"Not just those in the military, but for that matter, those throughout the civil rights movements of the '60s, and all that has been endured by so many people up until this point. And is everything right with our country right now? No, it is not. We still have a long way to go," Brees said. "But I think what you do by standing there and showing respect to the flag with your hand over your heart is it shows unity. It shows that we are all in this together, we can all do better and that we are all part of the solution."

After making those comments Brees was attacked, called a racist, and received a ton of criticism from the media and his own teammates. After speaking with teammates and friends and thinking about his comments, he had a genuine change of heart and took full responsibility for his remarks and shared a heartfelt apology. This is what he posted on Instagram:

I would like to apologize to my friends, teammates, the City of New Orleans, the black community, NFL community and anyone I hurt with my comments yesterday. In speaking with some of you, it breaks my heart to know the pain I have caused.

In an attempt to talk about respect, unity, and solidarity centered around the American flag and the national anthem, I made comments that were insensitive and completely missed the mark on the issues we are facing right now as a country. They lacked awareness and any type of compassion or empathy. Instead, those words have become divisive and hurtful and have misled people into believing that somehow I am an enemy. This could not be further from the truth and is not an accurate reflection of my heart or my character.

This is where I stand:

I stand with the black community in the fight against systemic racial injustice and police brutality and support the creation of real policy change that will make a difference.

I condemn the years of oppression that have taken place throughout our black communities and still exists today.

I acknowledge that we as Americans, including myself, have not done enough to fight for that equality or to truly understand the struggles and plight of the black community.

I recognize that I am part of the solution and can be a leader for the black community in this movement.

I will never know what it's like to be a black man or raise black children in America but I will work every day to put myself in those shoes and fight for what is right.

I have ALWAYS been an ally, never an enemy.

I am sick about the way my comments were perceived yesterday, but I take full responsibility and accountability. I recognize that I should do less talking and more listening...and when the black community is talking about their pain, we all need to listen.

For that, I am very sorry and I ask your forgiveness.

As I watched Drew during an interview, I knew he had authentically had a change of heart and was very sincere in his apology. I honestly do not believe Drew is a racist or that he was intentionally trying to cause division. He felt very strongly about the issue and he was simply expressing his thoughts and feelings without malice or hatred. His willingness to reexamine his beliefs and then change them is commendable and I believe his teammates and his friends fully accepted his apology. I also believe he was sincere in his statement when he said, *I recognize that I should do less talking and more listening... and when the black community is talking about their pain, we all need to listen.*

I'm reminded of a quote by Steven Covey in which he said, "Seek first to understand and then be understood." Drew took the high road and chose to understand a different point of view and in doing so he was able to understand that the protest was never about disrespecting the flag or the military. This is how we will change this country and our world, by being willing to understand another person's point of view and not being so rigid in our thinking that we make the other person wrong for their point of view. We must seek first to understand their point of view without judgment and even if we disagree with their point of view we do not have to condemn them when their view is different.

I realize these are just two examples of people changing their minds about race, but I think they are metaphorical of the change a lot of people are making about race relations. This change is being driven by Divine Intelligence and therefore it fills me with hope and optimism about the future.

I'd like to share another excerpt from my previous book *Shattering Black Male Stereotypes*. In the book I was speaking about the origin of stereotypes and I was sharing a theory I have, which is called the CWBS.

Here is the excerpt:

We must accept the truth that America is comprised of a diverse group of people who make up this great country. So, America is simply a reflection of the consciousness of the people who live here. Since the majority of people living in the US, for the most part, have been white people (except when they first invaded America), this country has what I call a Collective White Belief System (CWBS). The CWBS has controlled this country for a very long time, but as the country has become more diverse, the CWBS is losing its influence and power.

When people talk about institutionalized racism and white privilege, what they are speaking of is the CWBS. It is a belief system based on white superiority that goes back hundreds of years. Another reason for my optimism is the fact that each generation moves further and further away from the CWBS. During the '60s and the civil rights movement, the CWBS began shifting. The pioneers of the civil rights movement convinced enough white people that segregation and the treatment of people of color were wrong. This was no easy task. Changing the CWBS wasn't easy. That's why there were lunch counter sit-ins. That's why there was a march on Washington. That's why Dr. King's dream speech was so important. In order to shift the

CWBS, a tipping point had to be reached, and once it did things began to change.

So, what is the tipping point? There are some people who believe that once 51 percent of the population agrees on a new belief then that belief changes the collective consciousness of the country. Using the example of the civil rights movement, once 51 percent of white people changed their minds then the CWBS changed, and the civil rights movement was accepted and it changed the country.

Despite the apparent racial conflict that is still going on in this country, I believe that the CWBS is still being broken down and this country can achieve racial harmony. As a matter of fact, I believe it's inevitable. There is always chaos before creation, and the current racial chaos we're experiencing will eventually lead to unity. You may be asking why I believe this and you may believe that I am a pie-in-the-sky-dreamer, but it is my belief that there is divine order in the Universe and that power that is greater than myself is orchestrating the entire cosmos. This Divine Intelligence has an intention, and that is to create heaven right here on Earth and nothing can thwart that intention."

Another way to look at racism is to see it as a disease of the mind. When this country was formed, the majority of white people were infected with this disease. It was this disease that caused white people to believe they were superior to blacks. It was also this disease of the mind that caused white people to create a system of white superiority in which black people were enslaved and treated as less than human. As I reflect back over this country's history, I recognize how this disease still negatively impacts the lives of people of color even today. This is why it's important to continue a conversation about race and racism in this country. Although the overwhelming majority of people are not actually racists, the system which this country was founded on still has the residual effects of the disease of racism.

So what is the cure?

I believe the cure is a shift in awareness and understanding. Because of my belief in Divine Intelligence, I believe understanding breeds compassion and compassion breeds empathy and empathy breeds healing. What this country and the world needs more than anything is healing. Healing the minds and hearts of people around the globe is what the world needs and I fervently believe healing is possible. The reason it's possible is because of human evolution. Human beings are still evolving and evolution is the movement of Divine Intelligence. Therefore, as human beings evolve, so too does their understanding.

So what about you? Are you willing to evolve? Are you willing to increase your understanding so you can increase your compassion? Ultimately, it all boils down to each of us as human beings to shift how we see each other and recognize how we really are all the same.

There is a philosopher named Ken Wilber who says there are three primary worldviews that a human being can have.

1. Ethnocentric Worldview
2. Humancentric Worldview
3. Cosmocentric Worldview

An Ethnocentric Worldview promotes the idea that human beings are different and separate from each other because of race.

A Humancentric Worldview promotes the idea that all human beings are the same and they are intimately connected to one another.

A Cosmocentric Worldview promotes the idea that not only are all human beings connected, but everything in the Universe is connected to everything else.

Without question, the overwhelming majority of human beings see the world through an Ethnocentric Worldview. It is this point of view that drives racism. People who hold this point of view generally believe human beings are separated by ethnicity and it is this opinion that causes people to believe their race is the superior race. People who are racists take this worldview to the extreme. They believe their race is somehow superior to other races and it is this erroneous belief that causes wars, hatred, and division.

People who embrace a Humancentric Worldview are generally

open-minded and they can accept that all men/women are created equal and we are all born with certain unalienable rights. They do not see themselves as better than or less than other human beings, they simply accept that there is only one race, which is the human race, and they work towards bringing peace and harmony to the planet by not judging and attacking others who may have a different worldview.

People with a Cosmocentric Worldview (like me) believe everything in the Universe is connected to everything else. They are usually seen as the head-in-the-clouds, idealistic, liberal dreamers who are out of touch with reality. They are generally optimistic and have a deep reverence for life and all living things. Their focus and attention is on love, caring and understanding and they are pretty passionate about doing all they can to make the world a better place.

So which category do you fall under?

It's important to understand there is no right or wrong answer here. Simply be honest with yourself and if you are unhappy with where you are simply change your worldview. Of course this is easier said than done, but if you truly want to change your worldview, you definitely have the power to do so.

Let me reiterate my belief; I truly believe in Divine Intelligence and evolution and therefore I am extremely optimistic about the future of race relations. If you pay attention to the trajectory we are on as a species, I believe there are plenty of reasons for optimism about the future. With that being said, I'd like to close this chapter with a quote from Rob Siltanen written for Apple Computers.

"Here's to the crazy ones. The misfits. The rebels. The troublemakers. The round pegs in the square holes. The ones who see things differently. They're not fond of rules. And they have no respect for the status quo. You can quote them, disagree with them, glorify or vilify them. About the only thing you can't do is ignore them. Because they change things. They push the human race forward. And while some may see them as the crazy ones, we see genius. Because the people who are crazy enough to think they can change the world are the ones who do."

I like to think of myself as one of the crazy ones because I honestly believe I can change the world. I hope you'll join me.

"People often call me an optimist, because I show them the enormous progress they didn't know about. That makes me angry. I'm not an optimist. That makes me sound naive. I'm a very serious "possibilist". That's something I made up. It means someone who neither hopes without reason, nor fears without reason, someone who constantly resists the overdramatic worldview. As a possibilist, I see all this progress, and it fills me with conviction and hope that further progress is possible. This is not optimistic. It is having a clear and reasonable idea about how things are. It is having a worldview that is constructive and useful."

Hans Rosling

CHAPTER 5
Factfulness

After a very competitive election, the American people chose Joe Biden to become the 46th president of the United States. He replaces a man who in my opinion did his very best to destroy our democracy and created more divisiveness and hatred in our country than any other president before him. Of all of the things I believe he did, promoting the phrase "fake news", in my opinion, was possibly the most destructive. Whenever he was confronted with scientific facts, if he disagreed with them because of his own personal opinions, he immediately dismissed the facts as "fake news". By undermining facts and science, he perpetuated a multiplicity of conspiracy theories that far too many Americans believed were true. It has been said that the lowest form of intelligence is opinion (and of course we all have them) and this president only relied on his opinions and not science and that is the reason our country is in this temporary state of decline.

Take, for example, the Covid 19 epidemic. When the scientific experts warned him of the danger of the virus, he dismissed it and said it would magically disappear. When asked about global warming, he basically said he didn't trust the scientists and claimed global warming was "fake news". He also claimed he would be able to reopen coalmines despite the fact that coal production has been declining for decades and scientists agree that coal will be replaced by much cleaner alternatives like solar power and wind power. Even now, he refuses to accept the fact that he lost the election fair and square and is claiming there was a lot of voter fraud even though there is absolutely no evidence to support his claim.

When the leader of the free world is denying science and calling it fake news, it is impossible for our country to move forward. Our ability to innovate and create new industries and jobs relies on our willingness to embrace science and facts to allow us to grow as a country.

Fortunately, the American people were courageous enough to reject his way of thinking and chose to bring in a man who is willing to listen to science and facts as he works to move our country forward and overcome the wide range of challenges we are currently faced with.

One of the greatest challenges our new president will face is changing the narrative about fake news. It is important for us as a country to be able to listen to and be informed by journalists, scientists, and experts who know the facts and are willing to share them with the American people. Of course, not all journalists, scientists, and experts are going to be credible and should be listened to, but I have great faith in the American people and I believe we are ready to rise to the challenge of changing the "fake news" mentality that has been an integral part of the last four years of the current administration.

So, what do you think? Is the media filled with "fake news"? Do you believe our media can be trusted?

Remember the quote from the master teacher that said, "Your beliefs about a thing create your experience of that thing"? Well, if you pay attention to mainstream media you have probably concluded that the world is in steady decline and headed on a path of destruction and therefore you may be extremely pessimistic about the future. But is that really true? Is the world really in a state of decline? For some people, this is what they believe, and others (like me) believe there has never been a better time to be alive on the planet than right now.

So, the question is who's right? Truth be told, they are both right. But wait a minute; you may be wondering, *How can they both be right?*

The amazing thing about being human is our thoughts and beliefs actually create our reality. If a person strongly believes the world is coming to an end, you're probably not going to be able to get them to change their mind even if you provide evidence that is contrary to what they believe.

For example, have you ever watched two experts debate a topic on television? Let's take the topic of vaccines. There are some people who believe vaccines are the cause of autism, and therefore they are called anti-vaxers and they will not take a vaccine, while others believe vaccines are safe and have no problem taking them. There are expert doctors on both sides of this debate who provide scientific evidence to support their beliefs, so who is right?

Let me suggest that human beings have an insatiable need to be right and once they make up their minds, it is difficult if not impossible to get them to see things from a different perspective. Herein lies the origin of all human suffering and conflict. **Human beings love to be right!** As simplistic as it may sound, relinquishing the need to be right is the key to transforming your world and ours.

So how does a person relinquish the need to be right? Paradoxically, it's difficult and simple at the same time. To do so, a person simply has to be willing to change their point of view or perception.

Dr. Wayne Dyer once stated, "If you change the way you look at things, the things you look at will change."

Deepak Chopra was quoted as saying, "There are two ways to look at the world. First, you can view the world as primarily a dangerous place with only moments of safety, or you can view the world as primarily a safe place filled with only moments of danger."

I also love this quote from Steven Covey: "We must seek first to understand, and then be understood."

So, are you willing to change the way you look at things? Are you willing to have a different perspective about yourself and the world around you?

The intention of this book is to simply provide you with fuel for contemplation and hopefully allow you to "change your mind" about how you view the world.

Don't Believe The Hype Of The Negative Media

As I mentioned in the acknowledgement section of this book,

A few years ago, I ran across a YouTube video titled The Joy of Stats by a Swedish physician, academic, and public speaker named Hans Rosling (July 27, 1948 – February 7, 2017) To be honest, I really dislike statistics, but this video changed my mind. I was intrigued by the graphical nature of the video in which the presenter was explaining why the world was actually getting better and not worse through a series of visually stunning graphics displays. As I watched the video, I was filled with hope and optimism about the future of humanity and the video confirmed what I have always believed to be true; there has never been a better time to be alive on the planet than right now! In his book Factfulness, *Mr. Rosling provides verifiable facts and statistics that support my beliefs and his book provided me with insights and inspiration that are the basis for this book. Although I will not have the opportunity to meet Mr. Rosling, I wanted to acknowledge him for his brilliant mind, engaging speaking style, and scientific approach to explaining why the future is brighter than most people believe. I highly recommend his book!*

I enjoyed the book so much I wanted to share some of the things I learned that confirm for me that the world is actually getting better. Rest assured the information contained in the book isn't "fake news" but scientifically verifiable facts of what is actually happening on our planet right now.

To be honest and transparent, I normally do not like statistics because I know they can be misconstrued to say whatever an expert wants them to say; therefore, I want to highlight some of the "facts" from the book that give me reasons for optimism about the future.

The book begins with a simple test of 13 questions to gauge your understanding of the world. I'd like to ask those questions to see how well you answer them.

(Side note- These questions are taken from the book *Factfulness* by Hans Rosling with Ola Rosling and Anna Rosling Ronnlund)

Chapter 5: Factfulness

1 In all low-income countries across the world today, how many girls finish primary school?

*A 20%

*B 40%

*C 60%

2 Where does the majority of the world population live?

*A. Low-income countries

*B Middle-income countries

*C High-income countries

3 In the last 20 years, the proportion of the world population living in extreme poverty has . . .

*A Almost doubled

*B Remained more or less the same

*C Almost halved

4 What is the life expectancy of the world today?

*A 50 years

*B 60 years

*C 70 years

5 There are two billion children in the world today, aged 0 to 15 years old. How many children will there be in the year 2100, according to the United Nations?

*A 4 billion

*B 3 billion

*C 2 billion

6 The UN predicts that by 2100 the world population will have increased by another four billion people. What is the main reason?

*A There will be more children (aged below 15)

*B There will be more adults (aged 15 to 74)

*C There will be more very old people (aged 75 and older)

7 How did the number of deaths per year from natural disasters change over the last hundred years?

*A More than doubled

*B Remained about the same

*C Decreased to less than half

8 There are roughly seven billion people in the world today. Where do they live?

*A One billion in the Americas, one billion in Europe, one billion in Africa, four billion in Australia and Asia

*B One billion in the Americas, one billion in Europe, two billion in Africa, three billion in Australia and Asia

*C Two billion in the Americas, one billion in Europe, one billion in Africa, three billion in Australia and Asia

9 How many of the world's one-year-old children today have been vaccinated against some disease?

*A 20%

*B 50%

*C 80%

Chapter 5: Factfulness

10 Worldwide, 30-year-old men have spent 10 years in school, on average. How many years have women of the same age spent in school?

*A 9 years
*B 6 years
*C 3 years

*11 In 1996, tigers, giant pandas, and black rhinos were all listed as endangered. How many of these three species are more critically endangered today?

*A Two of them
*B One of them
*C None of them

12 How many people in the world have some access to electricity?

*A 20%
*B 50%
*C 80%

13 Global climate experts believe that, over the next 100 years, the average temperature will...

*A Get warmer
*B Remain the same
*C Get colder

Here are the correct answers: 1:C, 2:B, 3:C, 4:C, 5:C, 6:B, 7:C, 8:A, 9:C, 10:A, 11:C, 12:C, 13:A

According to Professor Rosling, the average score is only 40% correct answers. This test has been given to academics, teachers, and experts around the globe and yet the majority of people only get 40% of the answers right.

Why do you think that is? My conclusion is because we are so inundated with negative news most of us have a negative perception of the world. Professor Rosling broke it down into 10 Dramatic Instincts to explain why so many people fail the test and have such a negative viewpoint of the world.

Here is his list of the 10 Dramatic Instincts that all human beings have and my summary of what they mean.

1. The Gap Instinct
2. The Negativity Instinct
3. The Straight Line Instinct
4. The Fear Instinct
5. The Size Instinct
6. The Generalization Instinct
7. The Destiny Instinct
8. The Single Perspective Instinct
9. The Blame Instinct
10. 10 The Urgency Instinct

The Gap Instinct

According to Professor Rosling, human beings tend to divide things into two distinct groups and then imagine a gap between them; for example, good vs. bad, rich vs. poor, and us vs. them. This Gap Instinct is what causes people to believe human beings are separate and different from each other.

The Negativity Instinct

Human beings tend to instinctively notice the bad more than the good. This goes back to my original point that the amount of negativity we are exposed to shapes how we see the world.

Chapter 5: Factfulness

The Straight Line Instinct

When we see a line going up steadily, we tend to assume the line will continue to go up in the foreseeable future. Therefore, if we see a graph or statistics that show a trend in a certain direction, we think it's going to continue in that direction even though the line could bend and head in a different direction.

The Fear Instinct

If you watch mainstream news it's no wonder most people are filled with fear. The news generally covers topics like terrorist attacks, natural disasters, disease, murders, and violence. Yet, in reality, only 0.1% of all deaths come from natural disasters, 0.001% from plane crashes, 0.7% from murders, 0.05% from terrorism, and 0% from nuclear leaks.

The Size Instinct

Human beings tend to see things out of proportion. For example, if we look at police murders of black men, it's easy to conclude black men are being eradicated from society, when in reality the chances of a black man being killed by a police officer is less than 1% in comparison to other types of death.

The Generalization Instinct

To handle the overwhelming amount of information around us we usually will place things in categories to help us sort through the information. Unfortunately, these categories can become generalizations and we began assuming things that may not be true. For example, when we create the categories Us vs. Them, we might unconsciously conclude that anyone in that particular category is exactly the same as everyone else in that category, and therefore "they" may be perceived as the bad guy when in reality it may only be one person from that group.

The Destiny Instinct

We tend to assume that (a) the destinies of people, cultures, countries etc. are predetermined by certain factors, and (b) such factors are fixed and unchanging. As a result, we assume that other people, groups or countries will always behave in a particular way and are destined to succeed or fail.

The Single Perspective Instinct

A large percentage of people choose to see the world through their limited perception and belief systems. They hold fast to an idea that there is only one way to view the world and that way is their way.

The Blame Instinct

People who refuse to take responsibility for their lives will always feel like a victim. They will always point fingers and place blame on things like their parents, their race, their age, their educational background, and bad luck.

The Urgency Instinct

I believe there is a positive and a negative Urgency Instinct. A negative instinct would be to rush into a problem because we are afraid that there is no time and we may be too late to fix the problem, and yet we do not have any real concrete solutions. A positive Urgency Instinct is when we take the time to formulate a plan to tackle a problem that is extremely urgent and needs our attention.

It's important for us to recognize these 10 instincts and be willing not to automatically respond with them whenever we see news reports or statistics about what is going on in the world. Instead of going by emotions and feelings, take the time to add *Factfulness* awareness to whatever story you're watching and then come to your own conclusions.

I highly recommend you pick up a copy of the book and read it from cover to cover. It will definitely provide you with verifiable facts that should convince you that the world is actually getting better than most people believe. Rest assured if you read it you will come away from it feeling optimistic and excited about what the future holds.

I want to close this chapter with 20 Megatrends that Peter Diamandis shared on his blog. These trends fuel my reasons for optimism and confirm for me that, as a species, we are on a trajectory of unlimited abundance and possibilities for the future.

Be sure to visit his website and follow him on social media. His insights and science-backed facts will inspire you. www.diamandis.com

20 METATRENDS FOR THE 2020S

1. **Continued increase in global abundance:** The number of individuals in extreme poverty continues to drop as the middle-income population continues to rise. This Metatrend is <u>driven by the convergence of:</u> high-bandwidth and low-cost communication, ubiquitous AI on the cloud, growing access to AI-aided education and AI-driven healthcare. Everyday goods and services (finance, insurance, education and entertainment) are being digitized and becoming fully demonetized, available to the rising billions on mobile devices.

2. **Global gigabit connectivity will connect everyone and everything, everywhere, at ultra-low cost:** The deployment of both licensed and unlicensed 5G, plus the launch of a multitude of global satellite networks (OneWeb, Starlink, etc.), allows for ubiquitous, low-cost communications for everyone, everywhere—not to mention the connection of *trillions* of devices. And today's skyrocketing connectivity is bringing online an additional three billion individuals, driving tens of trillions of dollars into the global economy. <u>This Metatrend is driven by the convergence of</u>: low-cost space launches, hardware advancements, 5G networks, artificial intelligence, materials science, and surging computing power.

3. **The average human healthspan will increase by 10+ years:** A dozen game-changing biotech and pharmaceutical solutions (currently in Phase 1, 2, or 3 clinical trials) will reach consumers this decade, adding an additional decade to the human healthspan. Technologies

include stem cell supply restoration, *wnt* pathway manipulation, Senolytic Medicines, a new generation of Endo-Vaccines, GDF-11, and supplementation of NMD/NAD+, among several others. And as machine learning continues to mature, AI is set to unleash countless new drug candidates ready for clinical trials. This Metatrend is driven by the convergence of: genome sequencing, CRISPR technologies, AI, quantum computing, and cellular medicine.

4. **An age of capital abundance will see increasing access to capital everywhere:** Over the past few years, humanity has hit all-time highs in the global flow of seed capital, venture capital and sovereign wealth fund investments. While this trend will witness some ups and downs in the wake of future recessions, it is expected to continue its overall upward trajectory. Capital abundance leads to the funding and testing of 'crazy' entrepreneurial ideas, which in turn accelerate innovation. Already, $300 billion in crowdfunding is anticipated by 2025, democratizing capital access for entrepreneurs worldwide. This Metatrend is driven by the convergence of: global connectivity, dematerialization, demonetization, and democratization.

5. **Augmented Reality and the Spatial Web will achieve ubiquitous deployment:** The combination of Augmented Reality (yielding Web 3.0, or the Spatial Web) and 5G networks (offering 100Mb/s – 10Gb/s connection speeds) will transform how we live our everyday lives, impacting every industry from retail and advertising to education and entertainment. Consumers will play, learn and shop throughout the day in a newly intelligent, virtually overlaid world. This Metatrend will be driven by the convergence of: hardware advancements, 5G networks, artificial intelligence, materials science, and surging computing power.

6. **Everything is smart, embedded with intelligence:** The price of specialized machine learning chips is dropping rapidly with a rise in global demand. Combined with the explosion of low-cost microscopic sensors and the deployment of high-bandwidth networks, we're heading into a decade wherein every device becomes

intelligent. Your child's toy remembers her face and name. Your kids' drone safely and diligently follows and videos all the children at the birthday party. Appliances respond to voice commands and anticipate your needs.

7. **AI will achieve human-level intelligence:** As predicted by technologist and futurist Ray Kurzweil, artificial intelligence will reach human-level performance this decade (by 2030). Through the 2020s, AI algorithms and machine learning tools will be increasingly made open source, available on the cloud, allowing any individual with an internet connection to supplement their cognitive ability, augment their problem-solving capacity, and build new ventures at a fraction of the current cost. This Metatrend will be <u>driven by the convergence of</u>: global high-bandwidth connectivity, neural networks, and cloud computing. Every industry, spanning industrial design, healthcare, education, and entertainment, will be impacted.

8. **AI-Human Collaboration will skyrocket across all professions:** The rise of "AI as a Service" (AIaaS) platforms will enable humans to partner with AI in every aspect of their work, at every level, in every industry. AIs will become entrenched in everyday business operations, serving as cognitive collaborators to employees—supporting creative tasks, generating new ideas, and tackling previously unattainable innovations. In some fields, partnership with AI will even become a requirement. For example, in the future, making certain diagnoses without the consultation of AI may be deemed malpractice.

9. **Most individuals adapt a *JARVIS*-like "software shell" to improve their quality of life:** As services like Alexa, Google Home and Apple Homepod expand in functionality, such services will eventually travel beyond the home and become your cognitive prosthetic 24/7. Imagine a secure JARVIS-like software shell that you give permission to listen to all your conversations, read your email, monitor your blood chemistry, etc. With access to such data, these AI-enabled software shells will learn your preferences, anticipate your needs and behavior, shop for you, monitor your health, and

help you problem-solve in support of your mid- and long-term goals.

10. **Globally abundant, cheap renewable energy:** Continued advancements in solar, wind, geothermal, hydroelectric, nuclear and localized grids will drive humanity towards cheap, abundant, and ubiquitous renewable energy. The price per kilowatt-hour will drop below *one cent per kilowatt-hour* for renewables, just as storage drops below a mere three cents per kilowatt-hour, resulting in the majority displacement of fossil fuels globally. And as the world's poorest countries are also the world's sunniest, the democratization of both new and traditional storage technologies will grant energy abundance to those already bathed in sunlight.

11. **The insurance industry transforms from "recovery after risk" to "prevention of risk:"** Today, fire insurance pays you *after* your house burns down; life insurance pays your next of kin *after* you die; and health insurance (which is really sick insurance) pays only *after* you get sick. This next decade, a new generation of insurance providers will leverage the convergence of machine learning, ubiquitous sensors, low-cost genome sequencing and robotics to detect risk, *prevent* disaster, and guarantee safety before any costs are incurred.

12. **Autonomous vehicles and flying cars will redefine human travel (soon to be far faster and cheaper):** Fully autonomous vehicles, car-as-a-service fleets, and aerial ride-sharing (flying cars) will be fully operational in most major metropolitan cities in the coming decade. The cost of transportation will plummet 3–4X, transforming real estate, finance, insurance, the materials economy, and urban planning. Where you live and work and how you spend your time will all be fundamentally reshaped by this future of human travel. Your kids and elderly parents will never drive. This Metatrend will be driven by the convergence of: machine learning, sensors, materials science, battery storage improvements, and ubiquitous gigabit connections.

13. **On-demand production and on-demand delivery will birth an "instant economy of things":** Urban dwellers will learn to expect "instant fulfillment" of their retail orders as drone and robotic

last-mile delivery services carry products from local supply depots directly to your doorstep. Further riding the deployment of regional on-demand digital manufacturing (3D printing farms), individualized products can be obtained within hours, anywhere, anytime. This Metatrend is <u>driven by the convergence of</u>: networks, 3D printing, robotics, and artificial intelligence.

14. **Ability to sense and know anything, anytime, anywhere:** We're rapidly approaching the era wherein 100 billion sensors (the Internet of Everything) are monitoring and sensing (imaging, listening, measuring) every facet of our environments all the time. Global imaging satellites, drones, autonomous car LIDARs, and forward-looking augmented reality (AR) headset cameras are all part of a global sensor matrix, together allowing us to know anything, anytime, anywhere. This Metatrend is <u>driven by the convergence of</u>: terrestrial, atmospheric and space-based sensors, vast data networks, and machine learning. In this future, it's not "what you know" but rather "the quality of the questions you ask" that will be most important.

15. **Disruption of advertising:** As AI becomes increasingly embedded in everyday life, your custom AI will soon understand what you want better than you do. In turn, we will begin to both trust and rely upon our AIs to make the most of our buying decisions, turning over shopping to AI-enabled personal assistants. Your AI might make purchases based upon your past desires, current shortages, conversations you've allowed your AI to listen to, or by tracking where your pupils focus on a virtual interface (i.e. what catches your attention). As a result, the advertising industry—which normally competes for *your* attention (whether at the Superbowl or through search engines)—will have a hard time influencing your AI. This Metatrend is <u>driven by the convergence of</u>: machine learning, sensors, augmented reality, and 5G/networks.

16. **Cellular agriculture moves from the lab into inner cities, providing high-quality protein that is cheaper and healthier:** This next decade will witness the birth of the most ethical, nutritious, and environmentally sustainable protein production system devised by

humankind. Stem cell-based "cellular agriculture" will allow the production of beef, chicken and fish *anywhere*, on-demand, with far higher nutritional content and a vastly lower environmental footprint than traditional livestock options. This Metatrend is enabled by the convergence of: biotechnology, materials science, machine learning, and AgTech.

17. **High-bandwidth Brain-Computer Interfaces (BCI) will come online for public use:** Technologist and futurist Ray Kurzweil has predicted that in the mid-2030s, we will begin connecting the human neocortex to the cloud. This next decade will see tremendous progress in that direction, first serving those with spinal cord injuries, whereby patients will regain both sensory capacity and motor control. Yet beyond assisting those with motor function loss, several BCI pioneers are now attempting to supplement their baseline cognitive abilities, a pursuit with the potential to increase their sensorium, memory and even intelligence. This Metatrend is fueled by the convergence of: materials science, machine learning, and robotics.

18. **High-resolution VR will transform both retail and real estate shopping:** High-resolution, lightweight virtual reality headsets will allow individuals at home to shop for everything from clothing to real estate from the convenience of their living room. Need a new outfit? Your AI knows your detailed body measurements and can whip up a fashion show featuring your avatar wearing the latest 20 designs on a runway. Want to see how your furniture might look inside a house you're viewing online? No problem! Your AI can populate the property with your virtualized inventory and give you a guided tour. This Metatrend is enabled by the convergence of: VR, machine learning, and high-bandwidth networks.

19. **Increased focus on sustainability and the environment:** An increase in global environmental awareness and concern over global warming will drive companies to invest in sustainability, both from a necessity standpoint and for marketing purposes. Breakthroughs in materials science, enabled by AI, will allow companies to drive tremendous reductions in waste and environmental contamination.

One company's waste will become another company's profit center. This Metatrend is <u>enabled by the convergence of</u>: materials science, artificial intelligence, and broadband networks.

20. **CRISPR and gene therapies will minimize disease:** A vast range of infectious diseases, ranging from AIDS to Ebola, are now curable. In addition, gene-editing technologies continue to advance in precision and ease of use, allowing families to treat and ultimately *cure* hundreds of inheritable genetic diseases. This Metatrend is <u>driven by the convergence of</u>: various biotechnologies (CRISPR, Gene Therapy), genome sequencing, and artificial intelligence.

"Your task is not to seek for love, but merely to seek and find all the barriers within yourself that you have built against it."

Rumi

CHAPTER 6
Love

THE FIRST WORDS out of my mouth immediately after my divorce were, "I WILL NEVER GET MARRIED AGAIN!" Although it's been more than 30 years since I uttered those words, I vividly remember the feelings that caused me to say them. At the time, I was filled with sadness, confusion, fear, uncertainty, and even relief. I was sad because I was extremely close to my kids and I knew it would be really hard on them. I was confused because I didn't understand how and why my marriage had failed, and I was absolutely terrified of what would happen to my kids after the divorce. But I was also relieved because deep down inside I hadn't been happy in the marriage for a very long time and I honestly wanted the divorce but I didn't have the courage to do it.

After the divorce was finalized, I found myself in new territory. In some ways it was the first time I had ever really failed at something so major and life-changing and it was extremely difficult to deal with. I felt as if I had this huge letter D stamped on my forehead and I felt embarrassed and ashamed and I definitely felt like a failure.

As a result, I didn't date for more than a year. I threw myself into my work and did the very best I could to let my children know how much I loved them and missed them and would always be there for them.

After a year or so, I decided to try my hand at dating. To say my first dates didn't go well would be a gross understatement. They were absolute disasters, but I decided not to quit because I was really tired of being alone. After a few failed attempts I finally met someone who I really liked and we started dating. Things started off well. We were very compatible in most things and I really enjoyed her company. After a few weeks she decided to break up with me because she said I was emotionally unavailable.

I waited a few months and tried again and met someone with whom I had a lot in common. We dated for a couple of weeks and, once again, the relationship ended the same way. She said I was emotionally unavailable.

After a while, I became extremely frustrated and decided to stop dating. I concluded that relationships weren't worth the effort and was I really tired of the rejection and heartache they caused. This lasted for several months but eventually I started thinking about dating again. During that time, I had a conversation with a close female friend of mine that would end up changing my perspective on women and dating. During our conversation I was having a bit of a pity party and feeling sorry for myself. I was complaining to her about why women would say they wanted a good man but when a good man showed up, they would always leave. (Of course, I considered myself to be a good man.)

After listening to my rant for a few minutes, my friend looked me straight in the eyes and said, "If one person called you a jackass you probably shouldn't worry about it. But if two or more do you probably ought to get a saddle. Have you not noticed that you are the only common denominator in all of your relationships? Maybe it's not the women who are the problem, maybe it's you."

My initial reaction was to become angry and defensive. But I really valued my friend's advice and I decided to really think about what she had said. It then hit me like a ton of bricks. The women were not the problem, I was!

Sometimes there are moments that completely change the trajectory of our lives and this was one of those moments. As I sat there contemplating what my friend had said, I intuitively knew that I had to be willing to change if I wanted my relationships to change. It was in that moment that I fully understood exactly what Rumi meant when he said, *"Your task is not to seek for love, but merely to seek and find all the barriers within yourself that you have built against it."*

I had to figure out what internal barriers I had that were keeping me from experiencing true love.

In that very moment, I knew I had to take 100% responsibility for figuring out how to create great relationships and I was willing to do anything to make that happen.

After our conversation, I went home and started thinking long and hard about my past relationships. I then noticed a pattern and common denominator in all of my relationship failures. Each of my relationships would last approximately three or four weeks and they would end with each woman saying exactly the same thing, "I care too much about you to stay in this relationship and you're emotionally unavailable."

As I reflected back over my relationships, I recognized that each time a woman would say she "cared too much about me to stay in the relationship" I would become confused and defensive because it made no sense to me. Why would a woman leave someone who she said she cared about? I simply couldn't wrap my head around that. I was a good guy who was funny and smart, sensitive and nurturing; I was a firm believer in honesty and monogamy, and I was in extremely good physical shape and definitely not a bad-looking guy. As I sat there thinking about all the things I had to offer, all of a sudden I realized what I had been unwilling to address.

Each woman had mentioned I was emotionally unavailable!

But what the hell did that mean? I had no idea what being emotionally unavailable meant and I was really confused. But then I realized this was the missing piece of my relationship puzzle. If I could figure out how to become emotionally available in relationships then I should be able to create the relationship of my dreams.

With this new revelation, my journey of transformation began.

As mentioned in a previous chapter, that journey began with my willingness to go to therapy. What I learned through therapy was that my traumatic childhood was still having an impact on my life as an adult. All of the physical, emotional and sexual trauma I had experienced as a child had caused me to shut down emotionally as a defense mechanism to deal with the trauma.

Let me try to explain it with science.

As human beings, we all have feelings. Our feelings are the language of our Souls. Feelings are expressed as emotions, and emotions are simply energy in motion. There are four primary emotions/energies that we feel; mad, glad, sad, and afraid. These energies/emotions are energetic responses to external stimuli. For example, if something externally threatens us, we feel fear. If something external crosses our boundaries, we feel mad. If we lose something, in most cases we will feel sad, and if something makes us feel good, we generally will feel happy.

As children we are able to process emotions immediately and authentically. For example, if we're happy we laugh and smile. If we're sad, we will most likely cry. If we're afraid, we withdraw and move away from that which frightens us, and if we're angry we may throw a tantrum or strike out against what made us angry.

These are all normal reactions that every human being has.

As we feel these emotions and process them appropriately, the feeling or energy leaves the body and the feeling subsides. Here is an example… Have you ever watched two young children fighting one minute and then the next minute they are laughing and playing with each other as if nothing ever happened? This occurs because a child will feel the emotion, express the emotion and then release the emotion. It is exactly how a human being should express their emotions.

Unfortunately, starting at a very young age we begin suppressing and repressing our emotions, and when we do this, the emotion/energy stays trapped in our bodies. When a child is told not to cry when he/she is hurting, they begin to "hold in" their emotions, causing the child to begin to shut down.

I'd like to share my personal experience to explain the impact that childhood trauma has on a person's life and when I actually became "emotionally unavailable".

When I was six years old, I was separated from my mom and had to go live with my grandmother. When my mother dropped me off, I experienced excruciating pain and sadness that literally broke my heart. As I watched her pull away, I was screaming and crying at the top of my lungs and begging her not to leave. Of course, my grandmother insisted that I stop crying and said if I didn't stop crying, she would give me something to cry about. In that very moment, I began shutting down my feelings and emotions. This is the event that triggered most of the dysfunction in my life because, in that moment, I came to the conclusion that there was something wrong with me and that was the reason my mother had abandoned me. In psychological terms, the experience triggered my fear of abandonment, which ultimately created my fear of intimacy. It was my fear of intimacy that caused me to become emotionally unavailable. I was afraid of getting close to people because I was always afraid they would leave me. Therefore, I would always try to be "nice" to them to ensure they wouldn't leave. The downside of this is I completely neglected my feelings in an attempt to keep women in a relationship with me.

I ended up living with my grandmother for seven years, and during that time I experienced every imaginable type of abuse you can imagine. The trauma was so severe that I completely shut down my emotions by creating a defense mechanism of becoming a nice guy. By being nice, I could minimize the physical abuse I received from my grandmother. But in doing so, I lost the ability to express how I really felt.

As an adult, this led me to become co-dependent, meaning I always put other people's needs in front of my own because I had completely shut off my ability to feel. I did not know how to express anger, sadness, or fear and therefore I hid behind being nice and appearing happy even when I didn't feel that way. This is why I was emotionally unavailable, because I did not know how to authentically express how I felt.

It was my inability to share my deepest feelings with the women in my life that caused them to leave.

As a result of my commitment to become emotionally available, I was able to heal from my childhood traumas and remove my fear of abandonment and intimacy. By healing my heart and making peace with my past I was eventually able to find the woman who is absolutely perfect for me and we have been happily married for almost 19 years.

It has been a challenging and sometimes painful journey, but the love I feel on a regular basis, and the wonderful relationship I have with my wife, makes it all worth it.

Since the intention of this book is to provide you with optimism, I would like to share some of the other lessons I have learned about love and relationships that have allowed me to create the relationship of my dreams.

I've mentioned the importance of understanding that everything is energy; therefore, if you want to understand how relationships work, that's a great place to begin.

There is a guy named David Hawkins who wrote an amazing book called *Power Versus Force*. In the book he created something called a Map of Consciousness Scale.

Chapter 6: Love

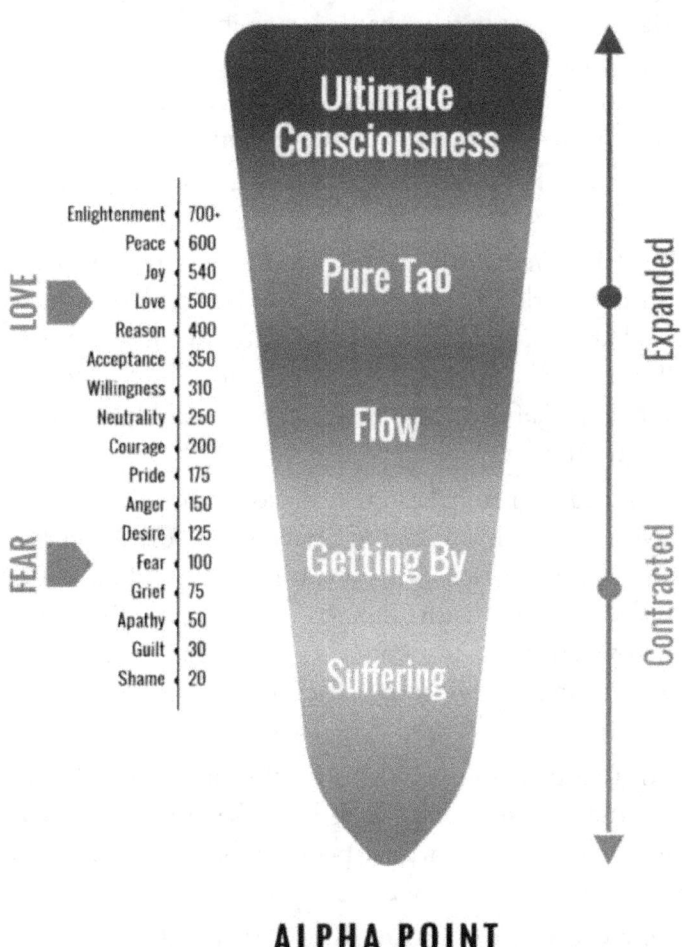

The scale starts at the bottom at 20 and moves up to 700–1000. Think of the numbers as vibrational levels. All human beings are energetic beings that vibrate at different levels and this scale will explain what those levels are. It's important not to judge the levels as good or bad; simply see them as levels of vibrations that you have complete control over.

According to David, most human beings vibrate at around 200. The point I want to make here is that it is possible to climb the ladder of consciousness to actually reach the 700 level or above if you choose to. In order to do this, you must be willing to get in touch with how you feel and recognize which level you are currently on.

During the time I was emotionally unavailable, I was probably vibrating around 20–50. I was so filled with shame from my traumatic childhood that I had very little confidence in my ability to be loved. As I did my inner work and climbed up the ladder, I became happy and secure in all areas of my life. If I had to rate myself today based on more than 25 years of healing and transformation, I'm easily between 600 and 700. My life is filled with inner peace, joy, and purpose and if I can get there so can you.

In order to create great relationships, you must begin by recognizing where you are on this scale and be willing to climb up the scale to increase your vibration. This is why you must be willing to do your inner work and make peace with your past. If you're holding on to past hurts and negative energy it is going to dictate your level of vibration and your level of vibration is going to dictate what you attract into your life.

If you want to attract someone who is vibrating at a high level you have to be vibrating at that same level. If you're vibrating at 100 you can rest assured you will only attract people who are vibrating at that level or lower.

The key to creating great relationships is first and foremost having a great relationship with yourself. In other words, it's important to have self-love first before you can attract love into your life. Pure self-love vibrates at around 500 so your goal should definitely be to reach that level so you attract that same level into your life.

If you're already in a relationship and want to deepen it, the key is to increase your vibration and your relationship will improve.

It all boils down to how you feel. Being in touch with how you feel and being willing to express how you feel is a surefire way to gauge where you are on this scale and to know how well your relationship is doing.

Once you know where you are and are comfortable with your level of vibration, next it's important to understand what exactly you are looking for in a relationship if that is what you're looking for.

So, let's imagine you're single and you decide you want to get into a relationship. Where do you start? Obviously the first thing you have to do is find someone to be in a relationship with, right? So, let me share a brief metaphor with you to provide some insights into choosing the right person.

I want you to imagine a beautifully wrapped Christmas present. As you look at this present you are filled with excitement and delight because the present is extremely beautiful. The present is so beautiful you want to show it off to your friends, so you take your present to a party to show it off. Once you get to the party all of your friends begin telling you just how beautiful your present is and you are bursting with pride.

After the party you take your present home and you can't take your eyes off of it. You can't even sleep because you can't get the present off of your mind.

The next day, you decide to take your present to work with you. When you get to work, your co-workers are all mesmerized by the beauty of your present. Once again you are bursting with pride as you show off your beautiful present to everyone.

One of your closest friends happens to be one of your co-workers and they come into your office and begin asking you some questions. "Where did you find such a beautiful present? How long have you had it? What's inside of it?"

Now you're beginning to get a little irritated because your friend is asking too many questions. You then tell your friend they should be happy that you're happy for having such a beautiful present, but your friend insists that you tell them what's inside the present. As a matter of fact, your friend grabs the present and shakes it just a bit. You become furious! "How dare you shake my beautiful present?" you say. You then tell them they do not have the right to question you about your present and even though the present sounded like something was broken inside you refuse to acknowledge that and you chase your co-worker out of your office.

After work you take your present home and set it on the table. You are still mesmerized by the beauty of the present, but you can't stop thinking about the sound you heard when your friend shook the package. A part of you wants to know what's inside, but another part of you is in complete denial and convinces you not to open it.

This goes on for a couple of weeks and the package has begun to lose its beauty. The wrapping paper is a little torn and the ribbon has fallen off and you aren't paying as much attention to the present anymore. You no longer take it with you and you've lost the feeling of love and joy that you had for your present. You then decide that it's time to look inside, and when you do, you find out that it is completely broken and it's something you didn't want anyway. So you take your present out to the dumpster and throw it in and the next day you start looking for a brand-new present.

This metaphor serves as a reminder of the importance of being willing to look past the exterior of a person and look at the interior. Of course it's important to find someone who you are physically attracted to, but if that is your primary focus you're looking in the wrong place. When seeking out a new partner the key is to connect with who they are on the inside instead of how they look on the outside. Just like the story, too many of us are more concerned with how our partners might look instead of who they are on the inside.

This is the reason the Map of Consciousness Scale is so important. If you are willing to look inside of a person and find their emotional level you are much more likely to be compatible if their level matches yours.

This was a lesson I learned as a result of some deep self-introspection and being willing to raise my level of vibration. The biggest lesson I learned from my divorce was that I had absolutely no idea

Chapter 6: Love

what interior qualities and values I was looking for in a woman. The first time I got married I was focused on the package and not what was inside it.

So, what exactly should we be looking for inside the package? I believe there are two things we must be looking for if we truly want to build a relationship that works.

1. Shared values
2. Identify our needs

When I got married the first time, I was 21 years old and I definitely didn't know what I was looking for. In addition to the emotional baggage I was carrying around, I was absolutely clueless as to the values I had and what my needs were.

I have come to believe that shared values are the keys to create lasting relationships. When two people share the same values around money, sex, religion, children, and ambition, they share a great foundation on which to build a great partnership.

So, the questions you must ask yourself are:

What are my thoughts feelings, and beliefs about money?

What are my thoughts, feelings and beliefs about sex?

What are my thoughts feelings, and beliefs about religion?

What are my thoughts feelings, and beliefs about children?

What are my thoughts feelings, and beliefs about ambition?

So take some time and think about these questions and then put your answers on some paper. Writing down your answers will give you some clarity on your values. Once you are clear on your values, whenever you choose to date someone have an honest conversation with them about what their values are and see if they match yours. If they don't it might be a good idea to look for another package.

Of course, this is going to take rigorous honesty on your part. You have to be completely honest and truthful with yourself about what you value most and make sure you do not compromise your values.

This is how you begin looking inside the package. This is how you begin to learn the essence of who they are. This is where true connection happens.

The second thing you must understand about yourself is your needs. As human beings we obviously have a lot of different needs, but in terms of relationships we have four primary ones. According to relationship expert Jayson Gaddis, the four primary needs all human beings have are the 4 S's.

Safety, Seen, Supported, and Soothed

Safety

Safety is about being in an environment in which you feel safe to express yourself openly and honestly. It means being comfortable to share all aspects of yourself with your partner without fear of criticism or attack. It also means there is never any threat of physical or emotional violence and you can simply be who you are with that person.

Seen

Being seen means we are acknowledged for who we are and the person we are with is able to see and appreciate who we are. It also means our experiences are validated and even if we disagree, our point of view is allowed without attack or judgement. Being seen also means being recognized for the unique human beings that we are.

Supported

Being supported means our partners are in our corners no matter what. It means they support us in pursuing our own individual interests and they give us the space to grow. Being supportive also means standing up and speaking out to us when our partners may disagree with us and want us to see things from a different point of view.

Soothed

We all want to feel loved and accepted and being soothed is the feeling we have when unconditional love is present. Being soothed occurs when we feel safe, seen and supported by our partners.

When these four needs are consistently met, love will blossom. Of course, this is probably easier said than done, but rest assured it is possible for you. How do I know this? Because I experience it on a regular basis, and if I can do it, so can you.

I'd like to close this chapter with 10 Keys to Creating Healthy Relationships. Be sure to read them carefully and apply them to your life.

Number 1:

Develop a healthy relationship with yourself. For most people, I can assure you, it is very uncomfortable for them to say, "I love myself." Why? Because for some people that may sound a little arrogant, a little cocky, a little narcissistic. The truth is, if you don't love yourself, you cannot love another person. It's not possible because all relationships begin with you. The first thing you have to be willing to do is create a healthy relationship with yourself. When you look in the mirror, ask yourself what you see. Do you see someone who's trustworthy? Do you see someone who's lovable? Do you see someone who's dependable? Do you see someone in that mirror you would want to be in a relationship with? Ask yourself that question honestly because that's where relationships begin.

They begin with you. If you want to create healthy relationships, start with yourself. Sometimes that means we have to take a break from relationships with other people and spend some time developing a relationship with ourselves. This may be uncomfortable or seem a little weird, but rest assured it is the first thing you must do. Too many times, we want to point our fingers at the people in our lives, but the fact remains that if we want to create healthy relationships, it always begins with the man in the mirror. We must take complete responsibility for our relationships and not blame anyone else except ourselves. Once we do this, we lay the foundation for great relationships.

Number 2:

Make relationships the top priority. In our culture and in our society, a man's job has basically been two things: protect and provide. This has been true since the beginning of time. Think about it. What was a caveman's primary responsibility? He was supposed to find a cave to keep his little cavewoman happy and warm, and then he had to go out there to find food and make sure he kept the dinosaurs from eating his family. Provide and protect.

Unfortunately, too many men are still trying to do that. They believe that if they just do these two things, then they will be happy. What we really need to do if we're going to make relationships our top priority is to connect; not just provide and protect, but connect. Connection takes emotions, and too many times men do not have the emotional awareness to connect, which is a major cause of relationship failure.

What we usually do is focus all of our attention on our jobs, our bills, our cars, our stuff, and our kids, but we aren't doing anything to connect in our relationships. We aren't doing anything to deepen our connection.

The sad part is that a lot of men will go through life and work at a career, raise their kids, and do everything they can to try to keep up with the Joneses. Then they get close to retirement and start asking themselves, "What am I going to do?"

As soon as they retire and they're at home with their wives on a full-time basis, it's total chaos because now they have to connect with their spouse, but they don't know how to do that.

If they would have only made relationships the top priority in their lives from the beginning it would have made their lives a lot easier in the long run. Be sure to make relationships the top priority in your life and you too will be happier in the long run.

Number 3:

Relinquish the need to be right. That's it! Let go of the need to be right! It's sad, but most people would rather be right than happy. What happens is they get attached to being right, which creates disconnection, and then they wonder why they're so unhappy.

Did you know that in healthy, connected relationships, two people never have to fight? "What do you mean, Michael? A relationship without fighting? That's not possible!" Yes, it is! I can promise you that it is possible, and here's how: you must make the distinction between fighting and conflict. They aren't the same thing. Fighting is about being right. It's about being more concerned with being right than being happy.

On the other hand, conflict is what occurs when you bring two human beings together who will always have different opinions and beliefs. There's no way you can avoid conflict in a relationship, but you can let go of your need to be right about the conflict, which will transform your relationships in an instant.

How many times have you had a fight over something really simple and all you had to do was say, "That's okay," and let it go? But then there was a part of you that took this firm stand that you were just not going to let her be right. We've all done it. It's part of human nature to want to be right. Guess what? It doesn't work in relationships. Relinquishing your need to be right will transform your relationships in an instant if you will just be willing to let things go.

At the same time, there will be some things that you feel very strongly about and you will choose not to compromise. You can do that without being attached to being right. You don't have to compromise your values in what's really important to you; you just have to be willing to say, "I don't have to be right. I'd rather be happy than right." When you do that, your relationships will transform immediately.

Number 4:

Be attentive to your partner. Being attentive to your partner means being in the present moment, fully aware of what they're saying, doing, and feeling. When we do that, we create connection. When you really pay attention to your partner and you're really concerned about what they're saying, connection is created. If you really want to create healthy relationships, you must be attentive to your partner; again, it creates connection.

Number 5:

Express affection to your partner. That doesn't mean you have to go out in the street and kiss your wife in front of a lot of people. Affection means that you're in some way affirming that you care about them by touching and acknowledging and possibly kissing them. Affection doesn't necessarily mean kissing; you can just touch someone and show affection. The key is to be comfortable making physical contact with your partner. Touching is a way to create physical connection. Studies have shown that infants that are held and nurtured and physically touched are healthier than babies that aren't. It's in our DNA to be touched and held. Expressing affection shouldn't be a big issue unless you're stuck in your ego, so let that go. Express affection to your partner.

Number 6:

Say, "I love you," and mean it. If you truly love someone, why should it be difficult to tell them? When you say, "I love you," be sure to say it from your heart, not your head. Say it often, and mean it every time. If you don't feel it, don't say it.

Number 7:

Spend quality time with your partner. You have to define quality time, but quality time means you move away from all the hustle and bustle of life, the kids, the jobs, the house, and all of that and you spend time where you're just hanging out. For some, it may mean just sitting on the back porch. For others, it may be going to a spa all day. You have to decide what it is, but it's important that you spend quality time where you're being attentive, where you're connecting with your partner. It's extremely important.

Number 8:

Loosen up, let go, have some fun. When was the last time you laughed with your partner? Just had a good laugh? If nothing comes to mind, something's wrong because relationships should be about fun, not just about stress and all the day-to-day challenges that we deal with. If you want to create connection, you have to have fun because, whether we realize it or not, we all have this playfulness inside of us. It's there. Too many of us have pushed it down so far we've forgotten what it feels like, but we have to bring that playfulness back up and have fun and recognize that it doesn't make you less of a person to do so.

Number 9:

Celebrate your victories together. Life is tough enough as it is. Just look around you. We have all these things going on in the world. Our one refuge should be our relationship and our homes. When you accomplish something or something positive happens in your relationship, you should celebrate that. It can be something as small as a hug or something as elaborate as taking your partner out to a really fine dinner because they got a promotion at work. The key is to recognize that you're in this together and you should be grateful that you have each other. When you overcome hurdles, it deepens your connection. Have some fun, celebrate your victories together, and acknowledge each other for being there for one another.

Number 10:

Count your blessings, not your problems. Too many times we focus all of our attention on what's wrong versus what's right with our relationships. When you focus all of your attention on what's wrong, guess what happens... Disconnection. If you're in a relationship, it may not be perfect, but you know this person is there for you and that's something to be grateful for. Count your blessings for what they do right. An attitude of gratitude goes a long, long way in deepening your connection in relationships. Make sure you're counting your blessings, not your problems. When you do that, I can assure you that connection happens and relationships bloom. That's just the way it works.

There they are, the 10 Keys to Creating Healthy Relationships.

I realize some of you out there are saying, "Okay, Michael, you've just shared ten keys to creating healthy relationships. I got it, but what I didn't get, what I didn't see, what I didn't hear you say, Michael, is anything about the sex. What about the sex, Michael? You didn't talk about the sex."

Here's a promise that I can make. It's actually a guarantee. I can absolutely, 100% guarantee that if you follow these 10 keys, if you create the connection I'm talking about in relationships, there is absolutely no way, *no way* you won't have great sex.

Here's why: too many times, we think that sex is about the physical act; in reality, making love is about the emotional and spiritual act. When you have your emotions involved and you have a deep connection with your mate, making love is deeper, more intimate, and more awesome.

Because when you really care about somebody, it's no longer just about physical sex. It's about sharing something, sharing a part of you. This whole process of connection is about moving past just having sex and making love. It doesn't mean you can't have some wild, crazy, passionate, physical love or sex. That could happen too. What I'm saying here is that we put so much focus on the physical aspect of sex that we miss out on the emotional and spiritual connection; when you do that, you cannot have great sex. If you have trust, commitment, honesty, openness, all those things in your relationships, your sex life, your love life, will work. I can guarantee you that. The question is, are you willing to accept it?

The question you're probably asking is, "Do these keys really work?" I know they do. How do I know? Because they work for me. If they work for me, they can work for you.

More importantly, I can honestly say that I have this type of connection with my wife. I have a marriage that works because I took the time to learn about me, I took the time to go through my emotional transformational process, and now it has allowed me to create this type of relationship. If I can do it, you can do it too.

I want to close this chapter with a story. This story is called "The Nine-Cow Woman". It goes like this:

Once upon a time, there were these two friends who loved to sail and had a beautiful ship that they sailed around the world in. One day, one of the guys decided that he was tired of sailing, and he wanted to settle down and get married.

So they go to this island, and the guy says, "I'm going to find the woman of my dreams on this island." His friend wishes him luck and they begin walking around the island to find the woman of his dreams. As he is walking around the island, he looks across the street and sees a woman who he immediately falls in love with.

He points to his friend and says, "There she is. There's the woman of my dreams."

His friend looks at the woman and says, "Excuse me? Not that woman standing across the street—because she's not that attractive."

"No, that's her. She's the one."

"Okay. I trust you, I wish you good luck, but I am going to continue sailing."

His friend gets on the boat and leaves the island. The other guy stays on the island. He gets a chance to meet the girl; they go out, they fall in love, and he decides that he wants to marry her. On this island, there is a tradition that before you marry someone, you have to go to the father and pledge a certain amount of cows in exchange for the daughter's hand in marriage.

On this island, royalty receive nine cows, while the average woman receives three or four cows. And so the guy goes up to the girl's father and tells him that he has fallen in love with his daughter and would like to ask for her hand in marriage.

When the father asks him how many cows he would like to give for his daughter, the guy says he would like to give him nine cows. The father looks a little surprised and initially rejects the offer because he doesn't think his daughter is worth the nine cows, but the guy refuses to give him anything less than the nine cows because that is what he feels the woman is worth.

The father agrees and the couple are married.

A few years pass, and his sailing buddy decides he wants to visit his friend. He comes back to the island, docks his boat, and begins walking through town. As he's walking through town, he notices a beautiful parade, and he also notices that there are a lot of beautiful women in the parade and on the island. For a brief moment, he even considers finding a woman for himself and settling down.

As he walks through town, he notices the most beautiful woman he's ever seen being carried through town. He admires her beauty for a moment then continues on to find his friend.

After a few moments, he finds his friend, and they embrace and begin to catch up on old times. His friend tells him that he met and married the woman of his dreams and that he is very happy with his life.

His friend then tells him about the beautiful woman he saw in the parade, and he tells his friend about all of the other beautiful women he has seen on the island.

As they are sitting there on the porch, all of a sudden the beautiful woman he saw in the parade walks up to them and says hello. She then walks over to the guy who stayed on the island and gives him a kiss.

The other friend looks at the woman then looks at his friend and asks, "Who is this?"

The friend replies, "This is my wife."

"But that isn't the same woman you pointed out the last time I was here."

"Yes, it is," he replies.

"It can't be! The other woman was not this beautiful."

Then the woman looks at him and says, "I'm the same woman you saw, and I'm sure I look different. If you're wondering what happened to me, it's really pretty simple. All of my life, people have been treating me as though I were a three-cow woman. Even my own father saw me that way. But my husband saw me as a nine-cow woman, and I simply chose to become the nine-cow woman that he knew I was."

The moral of that story is too many times we see people in our lives as one-cow, two-cow, or three-cow people. The truth is we're all nine-cow people; unfortunately, too many of us have forgotten that we are. Make a commitment to treat everyone as nine-cows, and I can assure you they'll become the nine-cow people they were born to be.

"The secrets of health for both mind and body are, not to mourn for the past, worry about the future, or anticipate troubles, but to live in the present moment wisely and earnestly."

The Buddha

CHAPTER 7
Health

I WANT YOU TO take a moment and see what comes to mind when I mention the word "vehicle". Did you think of a car, a plane, a boat? What did you think of? Now I would like for you to think about what might be considered "the ultimate vehicle". To do this, you must first define what a vehicle is. Dictionary.com defines a vehicle as: "any means in or by which someone travels or something is carried or conveyed; a means of conveyance or transport:. I define a vehicle in this context as: "something that moves human beings from one place to another."

Using that definition what would you consider to be the ultimate vehicle?

How about the 4.8-million-dollar Koenigsegg CCXR Trevita sportscar? Or what about the 4.8-billion-dollar History Supreme yacht made with solid gold? Or maybe you thought about the 150-billion-dollar International Space Station. Surely any of these vehicles could be considered the ultimate vehicle.

So what do you think? What comes to mind when you think about the "ultimate" vehicle?

If you asked me, none of these vehicles would make my list as the ultimate vehicle. For me, the ultimate vehicle is something that everyone can afford, and as a matter of fact, every human being already owns one. In my opinion, the ultimate vehicle is, without question, the human body.

What is truly amazing is 99% of the mass of the human body consists of six elements: oxygen, carbon, hydrogen, nitrogen, calcium, and phosphorus. They are worth about $576. All the other elements taken together are worth only about $9 more.

So if the human body is only worth $585 dollars why would I consider it to be the ultimate vehicle?

Remember when I said you are a spiritual being having a human experience? Therefore the essence of you is spirit and your body is the vehicle that moves you around from one place to another, so have you ever stopped to contemplate the beauty and complexity of your divine vehicle?

Let's look at just a few of the miracles of the human body.

Did you know that your body consists of approximately 100 trillion cells, which all came from the division of one single cell? Every minute 300 million cells die, but we produce over 300 billion new cells every day and our bodies are constantly repairing and rebuilding themselves.

Did you know that the human heart creates enough pressure to squirt blood more than 30 feet? Such pressure is needed to pump blood through 60,000 miles of veins and capillaries. The heart pumps six quarts of blood, circulating three times through the body every minute. In one day, your blood travels a total of 12,000 miles.

Did you know your stomach has a disposable lining? Your stomach gets a brand-new lining every four days. Strong digestive acids quickly dissolve the mucus-like cells lining the walls of the stomach. So your body replaces them, routinely, before they are compromised.

Did you know just three months into a pregnancy an unborn child already has fingerprints? At just six to 13 weeks of development, the distinctive whorls have already developed. Interestingly, those fingerprints will never change throughout a person's life. And your fingerprints are your own unique bar code indicating the true miracle you are.

Out of seven billion people on the planet, there is only one you! You are a miracle!

What separates the human body from every other vehicle is the Divine Intelligence that is within the human body. It is the only vehicle capable of repairing itself and it is also the only vehicle that gets stronger and better the more you use it. No other vehicle is capable of doing this.

It is this Divine Intelligence that causes a single cell to multiply and become more than 100 trillion cells. It is this intelligence that causes a broken bone to miraculously heal, your fingernails to grow, and a single sperm cell to fertilize an egg and create a new life. This is why I believe the human body is definitely the ultimate vehicle.

Let's use the metaphor that the human body is like a car. When you buy a new car, you usually begin by taking very good care of it. You keep it clean, you keep it filled with fuel, and you follow maintenance guidelines to keep it running smoothly. Whenever there is a problem with the car, it will let you know about the problem by turning on the check engine light or making weird noises, or maybe it begins to drive roughly. The point here is that the car will alert you to the problem and then it is important that you address the problem and get it repaired.

The human body does the same thing. It gives you signals to let you know there is something wrong with it. A few of the basic signals it sends are high blood pressure, high cholesterol levels, being overweight, and excessive stress and anxiety. These are all warning signs that the human body needs attention.

So now I'd like you to take a moment and think about your ultimate vehicle. Do you take good care of it? Are you paying attention to what your body is telling you? Is it time for you to get a checkup to see if your body needs repairing?

It is imperative that we take good care of our physical bodies if we truly want to be genuinely happy with our lives. Health is wealth, and therefore it is incumbent upon us to ensure we are healthy and wealthy by taking excellent care of our ultimate vehicle. With that being said, I'd like to share a few tips on taking care of your ultimate vehicle.

1. Get an annual checkup.

It is extremely important for people to get physical exams. People are hesitant to go to the doctor for a myriad of reasons, but the fact remains that getting a physical and early detection of illnesses improve your chances of overcoming those illnesses.

2. Watch your diet.

Yes, we love our food, and yes, we love to eat, but we must understand that there are certain foods that are detrimental to our bodies. Fried foods and high-fat foods are the leading cause of weight gain and disease. Make a commitment to yourself to eat healthier, and minimize the amount of food you eat.

3. Exercise.

You must understand that the human body is not designed to sit still; it is designed to move. It is the only thing on this planet that actually gets stronger the more you use it. Moderate exercise can extend your lifespan, help you lose weight, and help you ward off illnesses.

4. Maintain a desirable weight.

If you are overweight, make a commitment to drop some pounds. As you lose the weight, you will receive lots of health benefits as well as increased self-esteem.

5. Limit your alcohol intake.

Alcohol abuse leads to all sorts of health-related illnesses. It also leads to depression. Be sure to reduce your alcohol intake, and by all means, never drink and drive.

6. Stop smoking, and do not abuse illegal drugs.

Enough said!

7. Learn to relax.

There are several documented studies regarding the benefits of meditation. Learning to relax makes you more productive and focused, and it can help you eliminate the need for alcohol or drugs.

8. Laugh often.

It's been said that people don't stop playing because they get old; they get old because they stop playing. Never stop playing! Make it a point to laugh and laugh often.

9. Learn something new.

Learning should be a lifelong process. Studies have shown that people who keep learning throughout their lifetimes are less likely to experience Alzheimer's and dementia. Never stop learning!

10. Volunteer.

Believe it or not, volunteering your time and talents to help other people can actually be good for your health. Studies have shown that people who help take care of others tend to be happier and healthier than those who don't.

These are ten things you can do to help you take care of your physical body. Taking care of your body can sometimes be a challenging thing, but it is important for you to make this a priority in your life.

Sadly, we lose too many people to preventable diseases simply because they refuse to get a checkup. I understand how scary it can be to go see a doctor, but you must realize that early detection is the key to eradicating a lot of senseless deaths. In addition, we lose far too many people to alcohol-related deaths that could have been easily prevented.

I would like to challenge you right now to take a moment and think about your body. I'd like you to get a pen or pencil and do a simple exercise.

I want you to fill in the blanks:

If I would _____ right now, it would help me take care of my physical body.

I would like to _____ so that I will feel better about my body.

I am _____ pounds over my ideal weight.

I am committed to losing _____ pounds in 2021.

I am going to stop smoking, starting _____.

I am going to begin an exercise program on _____.

I am going to make an appointment to see a doctor by _____.

The one thing I do that I know isn't good for my health is _____.

In terms of my physical health, my goal for 2021 is to _____.

The one thing I can do right now to begin improving my health is _____.

The one thing that scares me about my body is _____.

I am going to _____ so that I can remove that fear.

    The key is for you to begin doing something to improve your health. Use these questions as a starting point to get the ball rolling and to support you in taking care of your physical body.

    As you begin making a commitment to taking better care of your physical body, it is important for you to understand that you have a Divine Intelligence within you that can and will support you in transforming your human body. Throughout this book I have mentioned the importance of developing an intimacy and connection with this Divine Intelligence and tapping into it is extremely important when it comes to healing the body. Whether you believe it or not, your body is actually able to heal itself from almost anything. The reason this is possible is because of Divine Intelligence. Unfortunately, most people rely on drugs and medications to try to heal themselves, but drugs do not deal with the causes of illness and disease, they only deal with the symptoms.

If you want to address the cause of most diseases you have to understand the point I made about energy. Everything is composed of energy and therefore you have an energetic body. Your energetic body is fueled by your thoughts and feelings. If you harbor negative thoughts and feelings they create negative energy within your body. These negative thoughts and feelings can definitely cause dis-ease in the body. If you harbor positive thoughts and feelings you can rest assured that you will be less likely to cause dis-ease within your body.

To fully understand the science behind this I'd like to introduce you to Dr. Joe Dispenza. (https://drjoedispenza.com) I've been following his work for several years and I attribute a lot of my good health to his teachings. Dr. Dispenza was a chiropractor who broke his back in several places and was told that he would never walk again. However, he was able to heal his broken back without surgery by tapping into the Divine Intelligence within and now he goes around the world teaching others how to access Divine Intelligence to heal their bodies.

Here is a post he wrote about his accident:

In order for some of us to wake up, we sometimes need a wake-up call. In 1986, I got the call. On a beautiful Southern California day in April, I had the privilege of being run over by an SUV in a Palm Springs triathlon. That moment changed my life and started me on this whole journey. I was 23 at the time, with a relatively new chiropractic practice in La Jolla, California, and I'd trained hard for this triathlon for months.

I had finished the swimming segment and was in the biking portion of the race when it happened. I was coming up to a tricky turn where I knew we'd be merging with traffic. A police officer, with his back to the oncoming cars, waved me on to turn right and follow the course. Since I was fully exerting myself and focused on the race, I never took my eyes off of him. As I passed two cyclists on that particular corner, a red four-wheel-drive Bronco going about 55 miles an hour slammed into my bike from behind. The next thing I knew, I was catapulted up into the air; then I landed squarely on my backside. Because of the speed of the vehicle and the slow reflexes of the elderly woman driving the Bronco, the SUV kept coming toward me, and I was soon reunited with its bumper. I quickly grabbed the bumper in order to avoid being run over and to stop my body from passing between metal and asphalt. So I was dragged down the road a bit before the driver realized what was happening. When she finally did abruptly stop, I tumbled out of control for about 20 yards.

I would soon discover that I had broken six vertebrae: I had compression fractures in thoracic 8, 9, 10, 11, and 12 and lumbar 1 (ranging from my shoulder blades to my kidneys). The vertebrae in the spine are stacked like individual blocks, and when I hit the ground with that kind of force, they collapsed and compressed from the impact. The eighth thoracic vertebra, the top segment that I broke, was more than 60 percent collapsed, and the circular arch that contained and protected the spinal cord was broken and pushed together in a pretzel-like shape. When a vertebra compresses and fractures, the bone has to go somewhere. In my case, a large volume of shattered fragments went back toward my spinal cord. It was definitely not a good picture.

As if I were in a bad dream gone rogue, I woke up the next morning with a host of neurological symptoms, including several different types pain; different degrees of numbness, tingling, and some loss of feeling in my legs; and some sobering difficulties in controlling my movements.

So after I had all the blood tests, x-rays, CAT scans, and MRIs at the hospital, the orthopedic surgeon showed me the results and somberly delivered the news: In order to contain the bone fragments that were now on my spinal cord, I needed surgery to implant a Harrington rod. That would mean cutting out the back parts of the vertebrae from two to three segments above and below the fractures and then screwing and clamping two 12-inch stainless-steel rods along both sides of my spinal column. Then they'd scrape some fragments off my hip bone and paste them over the rods. It would be major surgery, but it would mean I'd at least have a chance to walk again. Even so, I knew I'd probably still be somewhat disabled, and I'd have to live with chronic pain for the rest of my life. Needless to say, I didn't like that option.

But if I chose not to have the surgery, paralysis seemed certain. The best neurologist in the Palm Springs area, who concurred with the first surgeon's opinion, told me that he knew of no other patient in the United

States in my condition who had refused it. The impact of the accident had compressed my T-8 vertebra into a wedge shape that would prevent my spine from being able to bear the weight of my body if I were to stand up: My backbone would collapse, pushing those shattered bits of the vertebra deep into my spinal cord, causing instant paralysis from my chest down. That was hardly an attractive option either.

Maybe I was just young and bold at that time in my life, but I decided against the medical model and the expert recommendations. I believe that there's an intelligence, an invisible consciousness, within each of us that's the giver of life. It supports, maintains, protects, and heals us every moment. It creates almost 100 trillion specialized cells (starting from only 2), it keeps our hearts beating hundreds of thousands of times per day, and it can organize hundreds of thousands of chemical reactions in a single cell in every second—among many other amazing functions. I reasoned at the time that if this intelligence was real and if it willfully, mindfully, and lovingly had such amazing abilities, maybe I could take my attention off my external world and begin to go within and connect with it—developing a relationship with it.

But while I intellectually understood that the body often has the capacity to heal itself, now I had to apply every bit of philosophy that I knew in order to take that knowledge to the next level and beyond, to create a true experience with healing. And since I wasn't going anywhere or I wasn't doing anything except lying face down, I decided on two things. First, every day I would put all of my conscious attention on this intelligence within me and give it a plan, a template, a vision, with very specific orders, and then I would surrender my healing to this greater mind that has unlimited power, allowing it to do the healing for me. And second, I wouldn't let any thought slip by my awareness that I didn't want to experience.

At nine and a half weeks after the accident, I got up and walked back into my life—without having any body cast or any surgeries. I had reached full recovery. I started seeing patients again at ten weeks and was back to training and lifting weights again, while continuing my rehabilitation, at twelve weeks. I discovered that I was the placebo. *And now, almost 30 years after the accident, I can honestly say that I've hardly ever had back pain since.*

Without question his story is inspirational. What is truly inspiring is how Dr. Joe teaches others how to heal their bodies using Divine Intelligence. There are countless confirmed cases of people from all around the world who have healed themselves from a wide variety of terminal illnesses using his teachings and techniques. What is unique about his approach is how he uses science to explain and confirm how the body heals and he actually documents scientifically how and why the body can heal itself.

When a typical medical doctor experiences something they can't explain, they use a term called "spontaneous remission". So, if a patient cures themselves of cancer or heals a tumor, the doctor will use this term to try to explain it. In Dr. Joe's case, he is able to provide the science and explanation behind how the healing was possible and why miracles should be expected when you access Divine Intelligence.

In following Dr. Joe's work I have come to conclude that there are only five things necessary to heal your body. Number one is faith. It all begins with the belief that there is a Divine Intelligence within you that can heal your body. Number two is trust. Another word for trust is surrender. Surrender means you let go of all limiting beliefs and preconceived ideas about what is possible and you allow Divine Intelligence to work through you and with you. Number three is action. You must be willing to take action and work with Divine Intelligence for the healing to occur. Action can take the form of prayer, meditation, contemplation, reading books or participating in a seminar. Number four is patience. You must be willing to accept that everything happens according to divine timing. Therefore, you must understand that delays are not denials and have patience while Divine Intelligence works its magic. And number five is gratitude. Gratitude is an energy that attracts synchronicities into your life that will guide you to the next steps along your journey. An attitude of gratitude expedites healing and creates an inner peace and an inner knowing that everything is going to be okay.

As you read these words there are two parts of you that are

attempting to process what you just read—the part of you that doesn't believe what I've said and the part of you that does. The part of you that believes what I wrote can be referred to as your Higher Self, and the part of you that doesn't believe can be referred to as your ego. Your ego is your source of doubt and skepticism. It's that part of you that says, "I can't do that. It won't work for me. I've tried this woo-woo stuff before and it didn't work."

Your Higher Self is your connection to Divine Intelligence. It is that part of you that says, "I can do this!" It is that part of you that decided to read this book. It is that part of you that believes in possibilities, and it is that part of you that brings you clarity and confidence as you embark upon learning new things. Learn to listen to and trust your Higher Self. It may not be easy because your ego self is going to do everything it can to talk you out of believing it's possible for you. Do not pay attention to that part of you. Listen to the voice of your Higher Self and you will know when it is speaking to you by the positive feelings and emotions you have.

When you listen to your Higher Self, you will always feel positive emotions like joy, excitement, expectancy, elation, and inner peace. When you listen to your ego, you will usually feel negative emotions like fear, confusion, anger, uncertainty, and insecurity. Learning to trust that still small voice of your Higher Self should be your highest priority because it will guide you to always make the right choice for yourself in any given moment.

In summary, your body is the ultimate vehicle and it is your responsibility to take good care of it. Remember to nourish it with the right foods, exercise it regularly, and make sure that you take it in for maintenance on a regular basis. And most of all, give thanks to Divine Intelligence for providing you with the Ultimate Vehicle.

"There is no such thing as a lack of resources. There is only the lack of resourcefulness."

Anthony Robbins

CHAPTER 8
Wealth

I was born in the inner-city projects of Corpus Christi, Texas to a single mother with six kids. We were basically the poster children for poverty back in the sixties. I vividly remember living in government housing, receiving government food supplies and government-issued food stamps. Although I was very young, there was a part of me that really disliked being poor. I've heard some people say they did not recognize they were poor when they were little, but I am definitely not one of those people. At a very young age I knew we were poor and I didn't like it one bit. From a very early age I began questioning why we were poor and, even more importantly, how I could avoid being poor when I grew up.

Despite our financial situation, my mother instilled in me a simple idea. It was actually a mantra she repeated to me often and it is the lesson that propelled me to begin my journey to financial abundance. The most powerful thing she instilled in me from a very early age was her favorite quote: "If you want something badly enough, there is no one or no thing that can keep you from accomplishing it except yourself."

Since I wanted to become rich in order to avoid being poor, I took this message to heart and began laying the foundation for my journey to financial abundance.

Another influential person in my life was my grandfather. He was the guy who would share his wisdom and knowledge with me and to this day he is still one of the smartest men I've ever known even though he only had an 8th grade education. One of the most powerful lessons I learned from him was in response to a statement I made to him when I was 10 years old. The statement was, "Grandpa, when I grow up, I'm going to be rich."

I will never forget the loving, compassionate look on his face when I made that statement. He smiled and then picked me up and placed me in his lap and we began a powerful conversation that went like this:

Him: Wanting to become rich is a very good goal to have. How do you plan on becoming rich?

Me: I'm going to own my own company like JR Ewing. (JR Ewing was a fictitious character on a nighttime soap opera called *Dallas*. He was my hero growing up even though I had no idea what he did. The only thing I knew about him was that he was rich and I wanted to be just like him.)

Him: If you're going to become rich, I want to share two lessons you will have to learn to do so; are you ready to learn these two lessons?

Me: (My eyes grew wide and a smile came across my face as I focused all of my attention on what he was about to say.) Yes Grandpa, I want to learn those two lessons.

Him: The first lesson you have to learn if you want to be rich is how to think like rich people. The only difference between rich people and poor people is how they think. The second lesson you have to learn is how to listen. Rich people will tell you exactly how they became rich, so you have to be willing to listen to what they say. That means you have to be willing to read books about their life stories and listen to whatever they say about becoming rich. If you learn to do these two things you can become rich. Are you willing to learn these two things?

Me: Absolutely Grandpa. I will learn to think like rich people and I will also learn how to listen.

Even though I was only 10 years old, a part of me recognized that my grandfather had given me the keys to my success. By combining his two lessons with the lesson from my mother about no one or no thing can keep me from accomplishing anything I set my mind to, I had everything I needed to begin my journey to an extraordinary life.

Taking my grandfather's advice, I began listening to rich people so I could learn to think like them. When I was 13 years old, I read the book *Think and Grow Rich* by Napoleon Hill and it confirmed everything my grandfather had told me. In the book he talked about the first step to riches being desire, and I definitely had a burning desire to be rich so I knew I was on the right track. The second step he talked about was faith. Even though I was just a kid, I had a deep faith and an inner knowing that one day I would become rich. His fifth step to riches was imagination and I had an unlimited amount of imagination. I remember pretending to be in a corporate office with JR Ewing debating on multi-million-dollar business deals while in my make-believe office in a wooded area near own home. I would always pretend that I was already rich and my mind had no limitations as to the amount of money I could make. The eighth step to riches was persistence and this is where I excelled. I never quit. Whenever I set my mind to something, I always see it through. It is persistence that has allowed me to move through a wide variety of obstacles and adversities and ultimately reach my goals.

After reading his book, I felt prepared to take on the world and at the tender age of 14 I started my own company. I started a janitorial company without even knowing what it was.

Here is what happened:

I was on my way to school one day when I passed by a motorcycle shop and overheard two men arguing. One was the owner and the other was the mechanic. The mechanic was complaining about having to sweep the floors. He was screaming loudly that his job was to fix motorcycles, not be a janitor. After listening for a moment, I walked into the shop and walked up to the owner and told him I had a solution to his problem. I told him I was willing to sweep the floor if he would give me a job. He was intrigued by my proposition and asked me how much I would charge him. I told him to let me clean his garage first and then he could decide how much to pay me. He agreed and I told him I would come by after school.

After school I cleaned the garage and when the owner came in to see it, he was so impressed he said, "You're hired"! He then told me he would pay me four dollars an hour even though the minimum wage was only 1.60 per hour. I would work three days a week for two hours, which translated to 24 bucks a week, which was a lot of money for a 14-year-old back in 1974.

After a couple of months, the motorcycle shop began selling bicycles and once again the mechanic was upset because he didn't want to assemble them. I informed the owner that I knew how to put the bikes together and when I proved I could do it, he then hired me to assemble bicycles and I no longer had to sweep the floors. In addition, I was paid five dollars for every bike I assembled and sometimes I could assemble 10 per week.

This was my first experience being an entrepreneur and I loved it!

After working there awhile, I saved up enough money to purchase some really nice stereo equipment because I absolutely loved music. A friend of mine was having a party and wanted to know if I could be the DJ and his parents would pay me. Of course, I said yes and I launched my next business adventure. Before long I was doing parties, high school proms, and dances and I was definitely making a lot more money than I was assembling bicycles, so fortunately I quit that job and focused on my DJ business.

When I got to high school, I purchased my first car and learned how to install car stereos. I paid 400 dollars for my car and it had a 1000-dollar stereo in it. Installing car stereos became a hobby and pretty soon I had launched my third business venture installing car stereos for my friends.

While in high school, I attended a seminar that convinced me I could get rich selling vacuum cleaners. I decided to drop out of high school to pursue my dream of becoming rich. It was a very poor decision and I never sold a single vacuum cleaner; however, the lesson

I learned was that I was not afraid to take risks and that is a trait all entrepreneurs share.

I share these stories of my entrepreneurial journey for two reasons; first, to let you know that I have been dreaming about becoming rich since I was 10 years old, and second, I was chasing money and trying to get rich for all the wrong reasons.

After years of self-introspection and personal growth, I have come to understand the reason I was driven to become rich was because of a deep sense of shame. Psychologists call it "toxic shame" and it is an internal feeling that something is inherently wrong within a person's psyche.

My toxic shame began very early as a child when I noticed we were poor. I felt embarrassed and ashamed because the kids in my school would tease me because I would take egg mayonnaise sandwiches to school in brown paper bags that I was forced to reuse by my grandmother. I wore tattered clothes that were sometimes dirty and I usually wore passed down tennis shoes with holes in them. At a very young age I began internalizing these feelings of shame.

But the event that really triggered my toxic shame was when I was separated from my mom at six years old. Experts call the event "abandonment" and it was this event that shaped my entire sense of self. In my eyes as a six-year-old, my mother meant the world to me. I loved her more than anything. When she took me to live with my grandmother because of my sister's illness, my six-year-old brain came to the conclusion that there must have been something wrong with me and that was the reason she abandoned me. So I internalized that people who love you will leave you, and in an attempt to keep people from leaving me, I decided that being rich would keep them from doing so. Pursuing riches out of shame was extremely draining. No matter how much money I made or what material thing I purchased, I never felt truly happy. So, in my attempt to feel happiness I kept trying to buy more stuff and accumulate more material things, but it didn't work. I still felt inadequate and empty inside no matter what I accomplished or purchased.

There is a powerful statement that says, "There is a God-shaped hole in our Soul and the only thing that can fill it is God. If you try to fill it with anything else the hole only gets bigger." As a former Atheist, I really struggled with this statement, but because of my inner journey and coming to my own understanding of God, this statement makes perfect sense. I had spent most of my life trying to fill that hole with money, material things and accomplishments, but the hole only got bigger. As the hole got bigger, my feelings of shame grew with it. It wasn't until after my divorce that I decided to fill that hole by healing my emotional scars and doing my inner work, which led me to come to my own conclusions about God, which eventually filled the hole in my Soul.

This is the reason it is so important for a person to be willing to do their inner work and uncover any hidden beliefs or negative feelings that could be driving their behavior. In too many cases, we believe if we have the right job, the right partner, the right house, and the right amount of money in the bank we will be happy. But the truth is happiness is an inside job and you will never experience it by looking at things outside of yourself. You must be willing to look within; otherwise you will always go without.

Because of my belief in Divine Intelligence, I can now see how every event in my life has brought me to this particular point in my life. I can now see how my abusive childhood and feelings of shame challenged me to become intelligent and inquisitive and to have a great work ethic and pursue all of my dreams. I also see how my divorce was actually the best thing that ever happened to me even though it was one of the most painful events in my life. My divorce challenged me to uncover my unique gifts and talents of writing and speaking. If not for my divorce, I would never have become an author and a speaker. My own life experience confirms for me that every adversity in our lives actually brings us a gift and a lesson if we are willing to look deeply enough for them.

If you're interested in learning more about turning your adversities into allies I highly recommend you pick up a copy of *Adversity Is Your Greatest Ally – How to Use Life Challenges as Stepping Stones to Live the Life of Your Dreams.*

Another great book to read on this topic is *True Purpose: 12 Strategies for Discovering the Difference You Are Meant to Make* by Tim Kelley. In the book, Tim explains how every event in our lives is designed to help us discover our true life's purpose. The part in the book that intrigued me the most was his explanation of what he calls your "sacred wound". Your sacred wound is a unique event in your life that causes you pain and triggers a belief in you that there is something wrong with you. For me, my sacred wound was being abandoned by my mom. Although it was the most painful event in my life, it was also the most transformative because it set in motion a series of behaviors and events that shaped me into the man I am today.

In retrospect I can see how I used to believe money and material possessions would make me happy. Like too many people, I attempted to gain love and acceptance by buying people's love and gaining acceptance by the things I accomplished. Now that I have done my inner emotional work, learned to love myself unconditionally, and come to my own understanding of Divine Intelligence, I have a completely different outlook on what true wealth really is.

True wealth is not to be defined by how much money I have in the bank or by how many material things I own. True wealth comes from knowing I am connected to Divine Intelligence and therefore I have access to an infinite amount of wealth in a myriad of different forms. Since ideas are the Divine Currency of the Universe, I have an unlimited number of ways to make money while also making a difference in the world. One of my intentions is to eventually become a billionaire. Because of my belief in Divine Intelligence, I define a billionaire as someone who positively impacts the lives of one billion people and I am committed to accomplishing this within my lifetime.

So, what about you? How do you view wealth? I hope I have shared some fuel for contemplation that challenges you to reevaluate how you view wealth. I truly believe you have access to Divine Intelligence and that gives you the opportunity to create as much wealth as you like. The Universe is infinite and therefore there are no limits to the amount of wealth or the amount of money you can create in your own life, so it's up to you to decide what wealth means to you.

Don't Believe The Hype Of The Negative Media

I'd like to share 10 lessons I've learned that have helped me create my version of an extraordinary life and allowed me to feel "wealthy" in all areas of my life. Take some time to think about them and then apply the lessons learned to your own life to support you in creating your own version of wealth.

1. The key to building wealth is to uncover your deepest-held beliefs about money. One way to do this is by doing this simple exercise. Get a sheet of paper and at the top of the page write this:

   I believe money...

   Now get a timer or use your smartphone and I want you to set the timer for one minute. For one minute I want you to complete the sentence, "I believe money..." Don't think too hard about it. Simply write down whatever comes to mind. It's important that you be completely honest with yourself and do not try to monitor what you are thinking. Simply write down the first thing that comes to mind. Your list could look something like this:

   - I believe money is the root of all evil
   - I believe money is bad
   - I believe money makes people greedy
   - I believe money is good
   - I believe money can help me buy nice things

   The key is to keep writing for one minute. You should do this several times to bring up your subconscious beliefs about money. In doing so, you can then challenge and change those beliefs. Remember what I said earlier, "Your beliefs about a thing create your experience of that thing."

2. Be willing to examine the things you learned about money from your parents. Did you come from a poor family? Did your parents ever sit down with you and talk about money? Our beliefs about money usually start within our own families so it's important to challenge any negative beliefs you may have picked up from your parents and change them to positive ones.

3. Examine your beliefs about a power greater than you and your relationship with money. For example, if you believe in a God that punishes you and would keep you from accumulating wealth, that belief can keep you from making money. On the other hand, if you believe in a God of abundance and believe we live in an infinite Universe, the chances of you creating wealth are greatly increased. What are your beliefs about a power greater than you?
4. Spend less than you make. As simplistic as this may sound it is a key to becoming wealthy. As mentioned earlier, I was always trying to purchase material things to get people to like me and gain their approval. In a lot of ways, I was trying to keep up with the Joneses by buying things I really didn't need. Ultimately, I ended up with a lot of credit card debt, which definitely kept me from being financially wealthy.
5. Pay yourself first. Each month, when you pay your bills, you should set some money aside to go into a savings account. Getting into the habit of saving money is a surefire way to build wealth.
6. Create a budget and stick to it. If you really want to get a handle on your finances, a great place to start is to write down every single penny you spend for a full month. You will be amazed at where your money goes when you do this and it will let you know exactly where you may be able to cut back on some expenses. You must be willing to be honest with yourself about where your money is going if you ever want to figure out how to control your spending and support yourself with your savings.
7. Invest your money. Another way to build wealth is to allow your money to work for you by accumulating interest and value. You can accomplish this by investing in stocks, bonds, or basic savings accounts.
8. Contribute to a retirement plan. If your company offers a 401K retirement type program that matches your contribution be sure to take advantage of it.
9. Give some money away. This may seem counterintuitive since I'm talking about saving money, but rest assured it's just the opposite.

Giving money away through donations is a great way to make a difference and also make you feel good. When you feel good, you're actually able to make more money because you feel grateful for the money you have.

10. Start your own passion project. You do not necessarily have to start a business to generate additional income from doing something you love. I started writing books because I loved writing and eventually I was able to turn my passion into a business. You can do the same thing by finding something you love to do and then figuring out how to monetize your passion.

These are 10 simple things you can do to support you in building wealth. They may be simple, but rest assured they are not necessarily easy.

Your takeaway from this chapter should be there is no limit to the amount of wealth you can accumulate but you must be willing to examine your deeply held beliefs about wealth and make sure you do not have limiting beliefs that may be keeping you from creating the wealth you know you deserve. Remember we live in an infinite Universe, so develop an intimacy with and connection to Divine Intelligence and you can create as much wealth as your imagination can conjure.

I'll close this chapter with a quote from Jim Carrey:

"My soul is not contained within the limits of my body. My body is contained within the limitlessness of my Soul. I've often said that I wish people could realize all of their dreams and wealth and fame so that they can see that it's not where you are going to find your sense of completion. I can tell you from experience the effect you have on others is the most valuable currency there is, because everything you gain in life will rot and fall apart, and all that will be left of you is what is in your heart."

This is what true wealth is all about!

"Education is not the learning of facts, but the training of the mind to think."

Albert Einstein

CHAPTER 9
Education

To educate means, "bring out, lead forth, rear, to train." In our culture, when you hear the word educate you probably think of going to school and getting an education. In this chapter, I want to focus on education as a way of "bringing out" the intelligence that is already within you.

Throughout this book I have talked about Divine Intelligence and how every human being has access to it. Therefore, education is the process through which you access this intelligence. Traditionally, we go to school to learn facts and knowledge to help us acquire jobs so we can make money. In some cases, the more knowledge you have the more money you can make. As I see it, this is the reason so many educated people are so unhappy with their lives. They spend a lot of time, energy, and money learning facts about topics they really aren't passionate about in an attempt to make the most amount of money they can. When they don't make enough money, they learn more things, to get more degrees in hopes that it will increase their incomes and they think that will make them happy. In doing so, they disregard the very important lesson that Albert Einstein shared: *"Education is not the learning of facts, but the training of the mind to think."* In other words, they are learning facts and not really training their minds to think.

Let me be clear. There is absolutely nothing wrong with gaining degrees and getting a good education. Knowledge is power and therefore acquiring as much knowledge as possible definitely increases your chances of being successful in life. But if you think a degree is going to help you create a joy-filled, passionate life you are gravely mistaken. And isn't that what you really want? Don't you want to wake up in the morning full of energy, passion, and optimism? Don't you want to have a career that lights you up so much that it isn't really work because you love doing it so much? Don't you want to have a deep feeling of inner peace and confidence in yourself so you can handle any adversity or challenge with ease? Don't you want to have dynamic health in which your body feels good and you're physically fit and proud of your body? Don't you want to have rewarding and fulfilling relationships filled with intimacy and authentic connection? And of course, don't you want to have financial abundance, which simply means you have enough money that you never have to stress out over it and you can buy the things you truly want without worrying about how you're going to pay for them?

Isn't that what you truly want? Of course it is. It's what every human being wants. I call them the four pillars of a joy-filled life. They are: Inner peace, Dynamic Health, Great Relationships, and Financial Abundance.

Unfortunately, very few people attain these four pillars. Why is that? It's because they are focused on traditional education, which does not teach them how to achieve these four pillars. So, what is the key to attaining them? The key to creating these four pillars is to first be willing to build them upon a solid foundation. That solid foundation is Self-Awareness and Self-Actualization. And how does a person build Self-Awareness? Through Self-Education.

Self-education is the process through which a person becomes self-introspective and is willing to examine their deeply held thoughts, feelings, and beliefs about who they are. I shared some strategies on how to do this in chapter one. Now I'd like to share some tips on why self-education is the key to building an extraordinary life.

I want you to ask yourself this question: "What if that which we call learning really isn't learning at all? What if learning is simply remembering that which we already know?"

This is a very intriguing question and one that I have been thinking deeply about for a very long time. As I reflect back over my life and my entrepreneurial journey, I recognize I've always had this deep knowing that I wanted to be an entrepreneur. I have always loved reading books and learning about business and one reason I decided not to go to college was because I didn't want to be forced to learn facts about things I would never use and had absolutely no interest in. To me, it made no sense to have to learn about things that had nothing to do with business.

Whenever I read a book or take a course about business, something in me lights up. It's an intuitive feeling I get, like I'm remembering something I already know. Therefore, it's extremely easy for me to learn, and I enjoy doing it. Of course there are certain aspects of business that I really dislike and are more difficult for me to learn, but my love of business motivates me to learn some things I do not like because I know it will help me in my business.

Now take a moment and think about a subject you really like. When you are learning about it, is it easy? Does it excite you to want to learn more? When you are studying it, does time fly by?

Now think about a subject you dislike. Isn't it more difficult to learn? Does it bore you and you can't wait to move past it? Does time drag on while you're learning it and it takes forever to get through it?

Can you feel the difference? On one hand you experience positive feelings, and on the other hand you experience negative feelings. Positive and negative doesn't necessarily mean good and bad. They are simply energetic feelings we have as human beings. My point is the importance of educating yourself about topics that generate positive feelings for you because when you do, you are more than likely tapping into a subject that deep down inside you already know about. When you learn a subject that you are truly enthusiastic about, you are tapping into the energy of enthusiasm and enthusiasm can be defined as "energy of the divine". In other words, you are connecting to Divine Intelligence and when you do, you will have an infinite supply of creativity and ideas because ideas are the currency of the Universe.

The question now becomes why do so few people invest in their self-education?

I believe the primary reason most people don't is because we live in a society and culture that conditions us to always focus on things outside of ourselves. In other words, our materialistic consumer culture convinces us that external things will make us happy. We are bombarded with images that say if you love someone you should buy them things. We are told that having a diploma on the wall will validate us. We believe that having a large bank account will bring us inner peace. We believe that finding the perfect partner will complete us. So, what do we do? We strive for the American Dream, which is having the house, the wife, the 2.5 kids, the 401Ks, the family vacations, and the SUV in the driveway. These are all external things that in reality will never guarantee happiness. I'm sure you're aware of someone who has had all of these things and was still absolutely miserable. Speaking from experience, I was one of those people. I focused all of my attention on accumulating external things and it wasn't until I lost everything that I learned the lesson that external things really don't make you happy. They may bring you temporary pleasure, but ultimately they do not bring you internal joy.

The next reason (and most important one) people do not invest in their self-education is because it is extremely uncomfortable to do so, and as human beings we simply do not like to be uncomfortable. Self-education requires us to be willing to address a myriad of emotional experiences that were sometimes painful and most people are unwilling to experience that pain. But the purpose of self-education should be to heal that pain, and as difficult as it might be, we must accept that the only way out is through, and therefore we must be willing to go through whatever pain we may have experienced. (Be sure to reread chapter one to learn how to move through painful experiences.)

In summary, the two things that keep people from investing in their self-education are cultural conditioning and fear. Since you're reading this book, I'm sure you want to move past these things and you are ready to invest in your self-education, so let's dive in and gain some insights to help you do so.

According to motivational speaker Anthony Robbins, the true key to success is constant and never-ending improvement. I wholeheartedly agree with that statement and it definitely applies to self-education. Self-education should be a lifelong process that we commit to and our goal should be never to stop learning. Unfortunately, a large percentage of people stop learning after they graduate from school.

Here are some unverified facts about reading put out by a marketing firm called The Jenkins Group:

- 33% of high school graduates never read another book for the rest of their lives.
- 42% of college graduates never read another book after college.
- 80% of U.S. families did not buy or read a book last year.
- 70% of U.S. adults have not been in a bookstore in the last five years.
- 57% of new books are not read to completion.

I personally do not believe these percentages are true when it comes to books in general, but when it comes to books about personal development, I will assume these percentages would be pretty accurate. Generally speaking, people do not like reading books on personal development and self-education.

Since you're reading this book you are definitely not one of those people, so take a moment and acknowledge yourself for your commitment to your self-education.

To fully understand the purpose of self-education, it's important to accept that as a human being you have an infinite capacity to learn. There is no such thing as learning too much. There are some people who believe that as we age our ability to learn declines, but I completely disagree with this idea. The main reason I disagree with that idea is because of a phenomenon called neuroplasticity. Neuroplasticity is the brain's ability to reorganize itself by forming new neural connections throughout life. Neuroplasticity allows the neurons (nerve cells) in the brain to compensate for injury and disease and to adjust their activities in response to new situations or to changes in their environment. In other words, the brain acts like a muscle. The more you use it the stronger it gets.

Self-education is a way of strengthening the brain and creating new neural pathways to help us understand who and what we are as human beings.

Here is another way to look at it. I'd like you to imagine when you were born there were two aspects of your divine self. Try to picture this; when you are born, you have a big S self, and a little s self. Your big S self is your connection to Divine Intelligence and your little s self is connected to your conscious mind. As a child, you rely on your big S self to help you navigate the world. Your big S self is the source of your curiosity and imagination. It is that fearless part of you that is filled with infinite possibilities. Your little s self is the rational part of you that has one job and that is to keep you safe from harm. As you grow up, you are exposed to certain things that cause you pain and it is the little s's job to keep you from that pain. It then creates strategies to keep you safe. Unfortunately, these strategies also keep you from trying new things. Here is where the trouble begins. The little s self convinces us that the world is an unsafe place and we should not attempt anything that may cause us harm. Therefore, we stop taking risks and get stuck in things that are familiar.

For example, when a child is learning to walk, it pays attention to the big S self, which is encouraging it to try new things. It has no fear; it simply trusts itself to do something that it intuitively knows it can do. It will stumble and fall, but it will keep going until it is able to walk. During that time the little s self is in the background taking notes. It isn't influencing the child's behavior, but it is paying attention to anything that causes the child pain. It then stores this information in the subconscious mind.

As the child grows older, whenever it listens to the big S self and tries something new, the little s self steps in and reminds it about previous experiences that may have brought it pain and it convinces the child not to try new things. So now the child has to decide who to listen to, the big S self or the little s self.

This is the reason self-education is so important. Self-education helps us listen to the big S self. The big S self is the part of us that says, "Let's create an extraordinary life," and then the little s self will say, "You can't do that. You're not smart enough or good enough."

At any given moment this is the conversation every human being goes through. There is a part of them that believes they can accomplish amazing things and then there is another part of them that says no, they can't. There are literally two different voices in our heads at all times and one is the voice of the big S self, and the other is the voice of the little s self.

Which one are you listening to? By reading this book, you are definitely listening to your big S self.

Self-education is what allows us to hear and listen to the big S self. But how do you know the difference? How can you tell when you are listening to your big S self instead of your little s self? One way to do so is to pay attention to how you feel. The voice of your big S self will always feel positive because it is connected to Divine Intelligence. It will feel inspiring, joyful, expansive, open, and confident. On the other hand, the voice of the little s self will feel negative because it is disconnected from Divine Intelligence. It will also feel fearful, constrictive, closed off, and uncertain.

Self-education also helps us feel the difference. It teaches us discernment, which helps us distinguish between the two.

So how are you feeling right now? Do you feel as if you are listening to your big S self or your little s self?

It's been said that the mind is like a garden and our thoughts are like seeds. What seeds have you been planting in your mind?

So, let's talk about the seeds you are planting in your mind. Are they positive or are they negative? Remember, positive and negative are not judgments about good or bad. They are simply energies that will attract like energies. What you think about you bring about, so let's take a look at what you're thinking about.

Don't Believe The Hype Of The Negative Media

Let's start with television. What shows do you enjoy watching? Be honest with yourself and ask yourself how you really feel as you watch them. Next, take a look at the music you listen to. Is it uplifting and inspiring? Does it make you feel good? What about books and magazines? Do you read them? If so, what is the content and how does it make you feel? And what about social media? What types of information and stories do you follow on social media? And most importantly, let's look at the words you use and the conversations you have. Are they positive? Do they inspire you and others?

The Law of Attraction says "like attracts like" so therefore if you are focusing on positive things you will more than likely attract positive things and experiences into your life. On the other hand, if you focus on negative things, guess what is most likely to show up.

The goal of self-education is to help you connect with your big S self and help you focus on feeling good and having positive experiences in your life. It should be a lifelong process of constant and never-ending improvement.

I'd like to close this chapter with five things you can do to invest in your self-education and ensure you create a rewarding and fulfilling life.

1. **Invest in your personal growth.** In chapter one I gave some specific steps on making peace with your past and being willing to heal past traumas. This can include things like going to therapy, participating in workshops, reading books on personal development, and listening to audio programs dealing with personal development.
2. **Commit to a meditation practice.** Learning to meditate is possibly the most important thing I've done to improve the quality of my life. My meditation practice has given me a deep inner peace I could not possibly describe in words. I know of no better way to connect to Divine Intelligence than through meditation.
3. **Start a journal.** Journaling is a powerful tool to help you get in touch with your big S self and help you uncover deeply held subconscious beliefs that may be sabotaging your life. It also helps you get in touch with suppressed feelings and uncover erroneous thoughts

and beliefs you may have about yourself that may be keeping you from feeling joy. It's also a good place to begin a gratitude list in which you list all the things you are grateful for, which, in turn, will give you more things to be grateful for.

4. **Join a network of like-minded people.** It's important to surround yourself with like-minded people who are also committed to self-education. There is an infinite amount of online social groups, churches, and organizations that can provide you with support and encouragement, so do some due diligence and find a group that's right for you and join it.

5. **Develop intimacy and connection to a power greater than you.** You get to choose what path you take, but find a path that nurtures your Soul and feels right for you. Don't just follow a path that others are on; find a path that is right for you, and once you do, be sure to nurture that connection.

One of my favorite spiritual teachers is a man named Neale Donald Walsch. He is the author of a series of books called *Conversations with God* and I highly recommend you at least read the very first book in the series. There is a quote in the book that really resonated with me and it speaks directly to the intention of self-education. This is what he said: "Your purpose is to become the grandest version of the greatest vision you hold for yourself as a human being."

So, what is your grandest vision for yourself? Are you willing to become your grandest version? If the answer is yes, the only way to do that is through self-education and connecting to your big S self.

Are you willing to do this?

"Technology gives us power, but it does not and cannot tell us how to use that power. Thanks to technology, we can instantly communicate across the world, but it still doesn't help us know what to say."

Jonathan Sacks

CHAPTER 10
Technology

THERE ARE TWO things that truly excite me and give me optimism about the future. The first is my belief in Divine Intelligence and the second is my belief in technology. I have always been somewhat of a technology geek and as I observe the advances in technology, I am filled with excitement and thoughts of infinite possibilities about what lies ahead.

What I love about technology is that it does not discriminate. Technology does not care if you are young or old, black or white, gay or straight, rich or poor. None of these things matter to technology and therefore those of us who are willing to embrace it are the ones who will reap the benefits of emerging technologies.

Of course, there are some people who definitely do not share the same optimism. There are some who believe technology will lead to the destruction of the planet and humanity as a whole. I, however, do not share those beliefs and in this chapter I will explain why.

I believe the reason most people are afraid of technology is because they simply fear change. It's human nature to fear that which we do not understand, so people will immediately reject things they do not understand. But ultimately I believe technology will help usher in a new century of technological advances that will make the world a better place.

To put it into context, take a moment to think back to 1903 when two brothers who owned a bicycle shop decided they wanted to create the first airplane. Can you imagine the resistance they received when they said they wanted to create something that would carry people and fly through the air? I'm sure the "experts" and scientists thought they were insane. But what happened? They held on to their vision and ultimately proved the experts wrong and they changed the world with their technology.

Arthur Schopenhauer once stated, "All truth passes through three stages. First it is ridiculed. Second, it is violently opposed. Third, it is accepted as self-evident." I believe this applies to technology as well.

I am going to share some technologies that I believe can and will make the world a better place. There will be some people who may ridicule the technology and there are some who will definitely do everything they can to stop the technology. But, ultimately, I believe the technologies I'm about to share will become accepted as self-evident and prove to be good for the world.

Here is my list of the top nine technologies I believe will change the world for the better.

1. The Internet

Not since the printing press has a technology come along that has changed the world in such a profound way. The Internet, in my opinion, is the greatest technology breakthrough the world has ever seen. Through the Internet, the world has definitely become a connected global community. We are no longer restricted by racial and cultural boundaries or limited by geographical boundaries. In a lot of ways, it has connected us as one human family with the ability to connect with and communicate with anyone, anywhere around the globe. As the world continues to deal with the global pandemic, the Internet is allowing people to stay connected and in touch with loved ones no matter where they are. It also allows companies and universities to collaborate around the globe as they work together to create vaccines to remove the scourge of this awful virus.

Chapter 10: Technology

As companies continue to close as a result of the virus, a new surge of entrepreneurs has used the Internet to launch businesses that in a lot of ways are keeping our economy afloat. The Internet allows entrepreneurs to do business around the globe and, as a result, there is no limit to the amount of customers they can find or the revenue they can create.

2. Electric/Autonomous Cars and Vehicles

Few things are more exciting to me than electric cars. I am absolutely fascinated by the technology and the long-term benefits of electric cars should be cause for excitement and optimism for the future. First of all, electric cars are better for the environment. Since fully electric cars do not have an exhaust system, they do not have emissions; therefore they do not pump any fumes into the air, which means cleaner air and less greenhouse gases.

Another advantage of electric cars is they can be powered by renewable resources like solar, wind, and water power. Gasoline-powered cars are fueled by oil, which is a natural resource, but it isn't renewable.

Electricity is also cheaper than gas and powering electric cars typically costs one-third the cost of gas-powered vehicles. Since electric cars have very few moving parts, there is less frequent maintenance and need for repairs. In addition, electric cars are much quieter than gas-powered cars and therefore will reduce noise pollution.

These are a few of the mechanical advantages of electric cars, but what really excites me about them is their ability to become self-driving. Although the technology is still in an infancy stage, rest assured that autonomous self-driving cars and vehicles are the wave of the future. According to *Business Insider* magazine, they predict that in the future most people will no longer own cars because of electric rideshare companies that will be launching fleets of autonomous self-driving cars. It has also been predicted that traffic fatalities, DWIs and insurance rates will drop as more electric vehicles become available.

Currently, every major car manufacturer is launching or developing an electric car, so rest assured electric cars are the future. The primary downside of electric cars is cost, but as more companies commit to electric vehicles, demand will drive the prices down and pretty soon they will be available to everyone. The other obstacle for electric cars is range. Currently the average range of an electric vehicle is approximately 200 miles per charge, but as battery technology improves, so too will the vehicle range.

Speaking of cars, did you know there are now several companies that are offering flying cars? That's right! Flying cars! Cars that you can drive on the road and then fly through the air. They are predicting these will be widely available in less than 25 years and there are a couple of companies that have already received FAA approval and have begun selling their flying vehicles.

I'm reminded of the cartoon back in my childhood called *The Jetsons*. It was a futuristic animated show back in the '60s and now it appears that the show was simply a preview of what was to come.

Cars have come a long way since the first car in 1886 and I can't wait to see what's next.

3. Drones

What began as a toy for grownups has now evolved into a full-fledged industry that is changing the world for the better. Drones are being used to deliver medicines in places that are not readily accessible by car and are saving countless lives. They are being used to fight fires and to track endangered species of animals. People are using them to launch businesses and to record vacations and weddings. Rescue workers use them to locate victims of natural disasters, and farmers are using them to plant seeds and distribute pesticides and fertilizers.

There are even drone competitions where people compete for large purses of money by being the best drone pilot.

What's really impressive are the upcoming flying drone taxis, which are getting ready to be launched by several airline companies and ride-sharing companies like Uber. In the very near future, you will be able to call a flying drone taxi company and have them pick you up and whisk you away as easily as calling a cab.

4. Solar Energy

In a new report, the International Energy Agency (IEA) says solar is now the cheapest form of electricity for utility companies to build. That's thanks to risk-reducing financial policies around the world, the agency says, and it applies to locations with both the most favorable policies and the easiest access to financing. The report underlines how important these policies are to encouraging development of renewables and other environmentally forward technologies.

This is definitely good news for the planet. As more and more forms of renewable energy like solar are created, we move closer and closer to reversing global warming. While some people are against the so-called Green New Deal proposed by some politicians, the advancement of solar power and other forms of renewable energy are definitely the keys to solving climate change. As solar technology continues to evolve, and the prices continue to drop, it opens the door for innovative entrepreneurs to come up with new technologies and business models that will create new industries and jobs for the future.

5. Artificial Intelligence

I am definitely not a scientist and cannot explain exactly what artificial intelligence is and how it works, but I do believe it is having a major impact on the world. If you have ever used a smartphone or talked to an Alexa device you have used artificial intelligence. Without most people realizing it, artificial intelligence has already become ubiquitous in society and rest assured we've only scratched the surface of what's coming. A simple way to look at AI is to imagine a library filled with thousands of books. Now imagine you have all the content from that library installed in a computer program. Now imagine that you have a question that you need answered so you input the question into the computer and the computer is able to find the answer to your question. That sounds simple, right? You're probably thinking any

Don't Believe The Hype Of The Negative Media

computer can do that, right? But here is where AI comes in. AI is able to process all the content in the library and cross reference all of it and find the answer in less than five seconds. No matter what question you ask, if the information is available in the library AI will find it and be able to give you your answer. As computing power increases, it's like going from a library with thousands of books to a library of millions of books and still being able to process the information in less than one second.

Back in 2016, the world's first artificially intelligent lawyer named ROSS was hired by a law firm named Baker & Hostetler. ROSS is a piece of artificial intelligence software that uses the super computing power of IBM Watson to sort through millions of law books and court cases. It has proven to be effective and more law firms are now investing in the technology.

AI can be programmed for any industry. A lot of insurance companies are now using AI to put together insurance quotes over the phone based on this type of technology and they are doing it without any human input. The entire policy can be put together using only AI computers.

Of course, the biggest fear of AI comes from watching too many movies about it taking over the world. If you're a fan of the *Terminator* movies, you may remember Skynet. Skynet was an AI technology that became self-aware and then took over the world and produced a bunch of Terminator robots, which attempted to wipe out civilization.

I personally do not believe this will ever happen, but there are definitely some valid concerns about AI that must be addressed. No matter what, AI is here to stay and I believe it is positively impacting the world.

6. Robots

In the movie *I, Robot* with Will Smith, Will plays a detective who is extremely skeptical about robots and he takes on a murder case in which a robot kills its owner. In the movie, the robots were designed to be servants who were sworn to protect their owners and they couldn't figure out why this one robot would commit a homicide. The robot who was accused of murder turned out to be a very special robot and, unlike the other robots, it began to have human emotions and even vivid dreams. In the beginning, Will definitely didn't trust the robot and he believed it had committed the murder. But upon further investigation, he learned to trust the robot and was actually able to solve the case after realizing that the main computer with artificial intelligence had become self-aware and it had actually programmed the robots to do whatever it wanted them to do. It then began programming the robots to take over the planet. The reason the robot killed his owner was because his owner made him do it because he knew it would be the only way to stop the AI computer from taking over the world. He knew how much Will hated robots and he knew he would solve the case and figure everything out. With the help of the accused robot, Will was able to destroy the AI computer and reprogram the other robots and he was able to save the world.

It is a very enjoyable movie, and at the same time it perpetuates the idea that robots will turn against humanity and take over the world. So, let's look at the positive side of robots and robotics and remove some of the fear a lot of people may have about the future.

First of all, I believe the biggest concern most people have about robots is that they will replace humans and take away jobs. Although some robotics might do that, I believe robotics will also create jobs. As robotic technology progresses, there is going to be a need for repair personnel, software engineers, programmers, and even designers. As we usher in the decade of robotics, I believe a new industry could develop that hasn't even been thought of yet. Herein lies the reason why entrepreneurship is critical and it is necessary to work with robots and robotics to create new industries and job opportunities so that jobs lost to robots can be replaced with new and innovative new job opportunities.

Now let's look at some of the benefits of robotics and how they are impacting the world in a positive way.

Have you ever used or seen robotic vacuum cleaners? These miniature robots are programmed to go around your house and vacuum your floors for you. Based on some reviews I've read, they actually do a pretty good job and based on their popularity, you can be sure that there will be new and better ones on the horizon.

One of the fastest growing segments of robotics is robot-assisted surgeries for doctors. One of the most popular methods is called the da Vinci Surgical System. It allows surgeons to perform minimally invasive surgery with the help of robotic arms. The machine consists of four thin robotic arms inserted into strategically placed incisions just one to two centimeters long. The surgeon operates while seated at a console unit, using hand and foot controls and with a 3D, high-definition view of the surgical field. It can simulate an open surgical environment without the physical trauma of large incisions. The da Vinci System enables surgeons to perform even the most complex and delicate procedures through very small, precise incisions.

One of the coolest robot companies is called Boston Dynamics and they build a wide variety of different type robots. They build a humanoid type robot called Atlas, which is the world's most dynamic humanoid robot and is designed to take the place of humans in a wide variety of environments. (You have to see it to believe it so be sure to check out their website at www.bostondynamics.com) They can walk, run, roll over, and lift objects just like a human. You will be amazed when you see it doing gymnastics and jumping over objects.

They also have a robot called Spot and it's like a robotic dog. It walks around on four legs and it can be programmed to perform a wide variety of tasks. There was a video of one that had an iPad attached to it and it was going around a hospital and the doctor was interacting with patients to prevent the spread of the Covid virus. The patient could see the doctor and vice versa and they were able to communicate as if the doctor was actually in the room.

It was pretty cool to watch.

One of the most realistic and intelligent robots is a robot named Sophia by a company called Hanson Robotics. Sophia uses the most advanced AI of any robot and she can actually engage in real conversations with a human being. She can sense facial expressions and even understand human emotions. She has self-learning capabilities and can be programed to actually build simple electronics. She is so intelligent that in 2015 Saudi Arabia granted her citizenship to their country and she is the first robot to be recognized as a citizen. Do a Google search and watch her in action, she's pretty remarkable.

Speaking of female robots, did you know there are also robot sex dolls? As creepy as that might seem, it's true. There are very realistic robots that are designed not only to have sex with but to also learn how to communicate with humans and develop relationships with them. The AI within them helps them learn things like your mood, your favorite movie or color, and they can remember these things and communicate with you about them. Supposedly, their skin is supposed to be very realistic and they have simulated heart beats and warm skin. As creepy as that sounds, and I would definitely never want to have sex with a robot, I must admit that I am intrigued by the technology and would love to actually see one.

Overall, I believe robots will definitely contribute to society in a positive way. These are just a few examples of what they can do, but it doesn't scratch the surface of robotic potential for the future.

7. 3D Printing

Of all the technology on this list, 3D printing has the potential to have the biggest impact on the world. A 3D printer is a machine that is able to "print" different material to create an unlimited amount of products and items. Starting with the basics, you can take a roll of plastic and insert it into the machine. You then build the item using a software program on the computer. Once you've built the 3D model on the machine, you simply press "print" and the machine takes the plastic and begins layering it until it builds whatever item you programmed into it.

Currently, scientists are developing ways to 3D print human body parts. They have already perfected things like human ears, and they are predicting they will be able to 3D print human hearts in the future. Imagine the possibilities with this technology. What if they are able to

3D print human lungs, kidneys, or hearts? Imagine how many lives could be saved every year with this type of technology.

Another amazing use of 3D technology is construction. Companies can now 3D print an entire house including plumbing and electrical in just a few days made from concrete. As the technology improves and costs begin to fall just imagine going to third-world countries and being able to 3D print entire villages in just a few months. In just a few years, this could definitely become a reality. There is a company in China called WinSun Decoration Design Engineering Co. and they currently have the record for the tallest 3D printed structure, which is a five-story apartment complex. They are also known for 3D printing 10 complete houses in 24 hours and have even built an 11,840 ft. mansion.

Believe it or not, 3D printed cars are a reality.

Although you may not be able to find 3D printed cars at your local car dealership just yet, there are some very interesting concepts out there that do a great job of presenting the possibilities of 3D printing in the automotive industry. They even represent the first steps towards mass-produced 3D printed cars. Don't be surprised if you see a story about 3D printed automobiles. They are already being printed and they range from tiny economical mini cars to exotic style supercars.

The future for 3D printing is extremely bright. Companies are only limited by their imaginations of what can be printed. This is a technology I will definitely be following to keep up with the infinite possibilities that are being brought forth.

8. Gene Editing

One of the most fascinating and controversial technologies is a process called gene editing. It's called CRISPR and it has the potential to literally change the world for the better. Here is some information I copied from the website www.newscientist.com:

CRISPR is a technology that can be used to edit genes and, as such, will likely change the world.

The essence of CRISPR is simple: it's a way of finding a specific bit of

DNA *inside a cell. After that, the next step in CRISPR gene editing is usually to alter that piece of DNA. However, CRISPR has also been adapted to do other things too, such as turning genes on or off without altering their sequence. CRISPR technology also has the potential to transform medicine, enabling us to not only treat but also prevent many diseases.*

In other words, imagine being able to identify a genetically diseased gene like sickle cell and being able to remove that gene, repair the DNA, and thereby remove the disease. WOW!

The implications of this technology are mind-blowing. It has the potential of one day being able to cure a wide range of diseases.

9. Space Exploration

In January of 2004, NASA landed two rover vehicles on Mars. They were called Spirit and Opportunity. Their primary goal was to find out whether or not Mars ever had water on the planet. The mission was supposed to last only 90 days, but the rovers definitely exceeded expectations because the Spirit rover lasted six years and the Opportunity rover lasted 14 years. The mission confirmed the existence of water on the planet and without question it was a huge success.

In September of 2016, NASA launched the Osiris-Rex spacecraft to travel more than 200 million miles to rendezvous with an asteroid named Bennu. It took two years for the spacecraft to get there, and once there, it was able to retrieve some soil samples, which are going to be returned to earth.

These are just two major examples of the ingenuity and innovation of America's space program. However, they only scratch the surface of what's ahead in space exploration. Here are a few other examples of what to look forward to.

Asteroid Mining

There is an asteroid called 16 Psyche, which is located in an asteroid belt between Mars and Jupiter. NASA estimates that the minerals on that asteroid are worth 10 quadrillion dollars. That's a 1 with 19 zeros behind it. That's more than the entire economy of Earth. I'm not sure if they plan on trying to retrieve any of the minerals, but there are several companies now that are launching asteroid mining projects.

Moon Mining

Moon Express is a company owned by Naveen Jain. It was the first company to receive U.S. government approval to send a robotic spacecraft beyond traditional Earth orbit and to the Moon. Naveen said, "Our robotic spacecraft systems will collapse the cost of access to the Moon, introduce a new commercial paradigm for government missions, democratize lunar research and exploration, and blaze the trail for commercial space transportation and exploration beyond Earth's orbit."

Space Travel Tourism

Virgin Galactic is now offering sub-orbital flights in which customers will be able to enter the lower fringes of space and float in zero gravity and take in spectacular views of our amazing planet. Tickets start at $250,000, but if it works and takes off, rest assured there will be more competition, which will definitely drive down the cost. Sign me up baby! I would love to go.

There are some people who believe space exploration is a waste of money and we should focus on social problems on Earth before we begin exploring space. I completely disagree. It is absolutely imperative that we have a space program because it not only allows us to learn about space, it also gives us an opportunity to develop a contingency plan just in case Earth becomes uninhabitable. Who knows what will happen in the future, so why not begin thinking about worst-case scenarios so we are prepared just in case?

As an optimist, these technologies give me reason for hope and excitement. I have great faith in humanity and, ultimately, I believe we will rise above all of our challenges. Technology can definitely lead the way, but we must remember not to place it before our humanity.

Always remember, people first; technology second!

"So, the path of the co-creator is to be awakened spiritually within, which then turns into your own deeper life purpose, which then makes you want to reach out and touch others in a way that expresses self and really evolves our communities and our world. Certainly, we can't do that unless we activate ourselves first. That's why, for me, emergence is the shift from ego to essence. That is so important."

– Barbara Marx Hubbard

WHAT'S NEXT?

Now that you've come to the end of the book it's time for you to ask yourself what's next. What do you plan on doing with the insights you've learned from this book? How can the new insights support you in improving the quality of your life? My hope is that you will be able to take the lessons learned and apply them to your life so that your life can become extraordinary. If nothing else, I hope this book has provided you with some reasons for optimism and given you a new perspective about yourself and the world around you.

Do not forget about the four pillars of a joy-filled life: Inner Peace, Dynamic Health, Great Relationships, and Financial Abundance. Make it a priority to invest in your self-education so you can experience these four pillars for yourself. Once you achieve them, be sure to reach back and support someone else in attaining them. A great way to do that is to share a copy of this book with them. Use the book as a guide to engage in conversations with others about the reasons for optimism you learned from this book.

Become an optimist!

Be positive!

Have fun!

Enjoy life!

I would be remiss if I didn't conclude this book with some thoughts about Divine Intelligence, so I'd like to share some fuel for contemplation for you to think about.

In chapter 7, I mentioned that the human body is the world's greatest vehicle, but did you know that the human body is also a metaphor for the entire Universe?

Think about it!

The human body has major organs like the brain, the heart, the lungs, the arteries, and trillions of cells that replenish themselves on a daily basis. You do not have to think about or tell your organs what to do; they intuitively know exactly what their job is. A red blood cell knows that its job is to transport oxygen to the body's tissues in exchange for carbon dioxide, which is carried to and eliminated by the lungs. A white blood cell knows it is a part of the body's immune system and its job is to help the body fight off infection and disease. But how do the cells know this? It's simple; they are guided by Divine Intelligence.

Now think about the Universe. It has planets, which are like the body, and it has countries, which are like its organs. It also has people, who are like its cells. Like the cells in the human body, people also have unique jobs they are supposed to do. Each human being has Divine Intelligence within them and when they learn to listen to it and trust it, it will guide them to their specific job.

In human terms, it's called your Divine Purpose and whether you believe it or not, you have one. Your job is to figure out what your Divine Purpose is.

If you follow some of the guidance in this book, I believe it can help you find your Divine Purpose. Unfortunately, I cannot tell you exactly how to find yours because every human being is unique and different and every path is a different path. What I can offer you is a key that might help you locate your purpose. That key is you will find your purpose when you figure out what you are good at and what you love to do. When you figure that out and then find a way to use that which you love to do to make the world a better place, you will have found your purpose.

Here are three ways to know if you are doing what you love.

1. *If you are doing what you love you will do it without thought of*

compensation. This does not mean you can't make money doing it; it means you love doing it so much you really do not care if you make any money. You do it for the pure joy of doing it and it feels good to do it.

2. *When you are doing what you love, time literally disappears.* Everyone has had experiences in which time literally flies by. As a writer, I can sit at my computer for eight hours writing and it seems as if 10 minutes have gone by. This is what happens when you do what you love.

3. *When you do what you love, you'll want to share it with others.* There is a joy that comes from sharing what you love with other people. When you put your heart and soul into something and then watch other people smile or enjoy what you've done, it will make you love what you do even more.

Now think about something you love doing and see if these three things hold true. If they do, you have found what you love to do. But here is a word of caution. If you love doing something but you're really not good at it, rest assured you have not found your purpose. When you find your purpose, you will love it and you will be good at it.

Once you find it, figure out how to serve others with your gifts and then you will have found your Divine Purpose.

Once you find your purpose you will be like a divine cell in the body of God. Ultimately, the job of every cell is to help heal the body and that is what you will be doing by sharing your gifts and talents.

Because of my belief in Divine Intelligence, I believe every human being is just like a cell in the body. Throughout history, Divine Intelligence has inspired certain human beings to help expedite the healing of the body. We generally look up to these individuals as spiritual masters, but ultimately they are just cells in the body just like you are.

You are a divine and unique expression of Divine Intelligence. Your job is to connect with it and assist it in healing the body of humanity. When you share your gifts with the world, and help make it a better place, that is exactly what you are doing, and I can assure you the joy you will feel will light you up from the inside and you will be able to light up the world.

So, remember these words from Rumi: "If light is in your heart, you will find your way home."

Be sure to find your way home.

I'll see you there!

Michael

BIO

Coach Michael Taylor *is an entrepreneur, author, motivational speaker, and radio show host who has dedicated his life to empowering men and women to reach their full potential. He knows first-hand how to overcome adversity and build a rewarding and fulfilling life. Taylor's sharing his knowledge and wisdom with others to support them in creating the life of their dreams.*

He's neither a stranger to adversity nor challenges. He was born in the inner-city projects of Corpus Christi, Texas to a single mother with six children. Although he dropped out of high school in the eleventh grade, his commitment to living an extraordinary life supported him in defying the odds.

With persistence, patience, and perseverance, he was able to climb the corporate ladder of success. Taylor has become a very successful mid-level manager of a multi-million dollar building supply center at the tender young age of twenty-one. After approximately six years, he was then faced with another set of challenges as he experienced the pain and humiliation of divorce, bankruptcy and foreclosure, depression and homeless for two years living out of his car.

Bankrupt and alone, he committed to rebuilding his life which propelled him to begin a twenty-five-year inner journey of personal transformation. This resulted in him discovering his true self and his passions for living. As a result, he's now been happily married for nineteen years, and living his version of an extraordinary life while being in service to others. Through his books, lectures, and radio program, he now coaches others on how to become genuinely happy with their lives while living the lives they were born to live.

Websites:

www.coachmichaeltaylor.com
www.adversityisyourgreatestally.com
www.creationpublishing.com
www.anewconversationwithmen.com
www.shatteringblackmalestereotypes.com

Contact us:

Email: mtaylor@coachmichaeltaylor.com
Phone: 877-255-3588

Social Media

Facebook@coachmichaeltaylor
Instagram@coachmichaeltaylor
Twitter@coachmichaelt
LinkedIn@coachmichaeltaylor

www.ingramcontent.com/pod-product-compliance
Lightning Source LLC
Chambersburg PA
CBHW070559010526
44118CB00012B/1379